CM0092096Z

WALKING IN THE LANGUEDOC

by

John Cross

CICERONE PRESS
MILNTHORPE CUMBRIA LA7 7PY
www.cicerone.co.uk

©2001 J. Cross
ISBN 1 85284 309 8
A catalogue for this book is available from the British Library.

ACKNOWLEDGEMENTS

I would like to thank Jonathan Williams of Cicerone Press for persuading me to write this book and for his very helpful advice in putting it together. I am also hugely grateful to my wife, Sarah, for sharing all these walks with me, offering suggestions for the text, proof-reading and generally being very patient.

Advice to Readers

Readers are advised that while every effort is taken by the author to ensure the accuracy of this guidebook, changes can occur which may affect the contents. It is advisable to check locally on transport, accommodation, shops, etc, but even rights of way can be altered.

The publisher would welcome notes of any such changes.

Cover photo: Walking through the Cirque de Mourèze (Walks 25 and 26)

CONTENTS

KEY TO MAPS

ROUTE

SECONDARY ROUTE

MAIN ROAD

MINOR ROAD

VIEWING PLATFORM

QUARRY

WINDMILL

REFUGE

RIVER OR STREAM

LAKE

BUILDING

CHAPEL

WOOD (DECIDUOUS)

WOOD (EVERGREEN)

SUMMIT

CLINIC

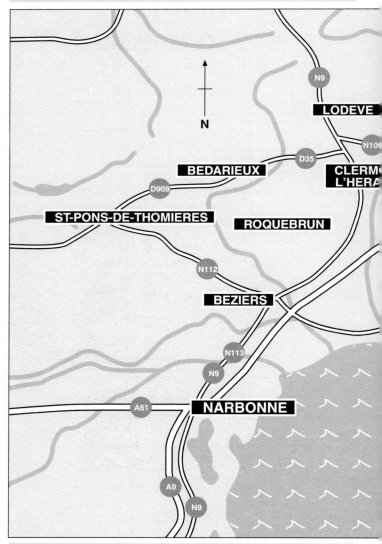

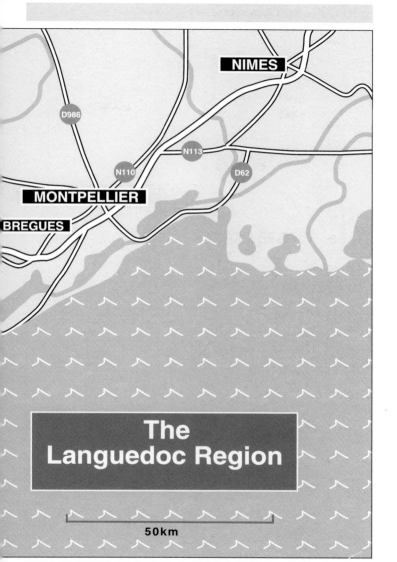

The
Languedoc Region

50km

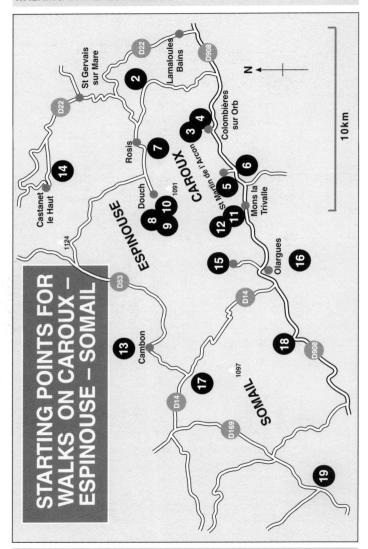

STARTING POINTS FOR WALKS ON CAROUX – ESPINOUSE – SOMAIL

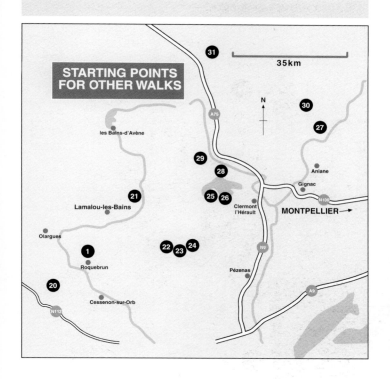

STARTING POINTS
FOR OTHER WALKS

35km

N

31

30

27

les Bains-d'Avène

29

28

25 26

Aniane

Gignac

21

Lamalou-les-Bains

Clermont
l'Hérault

MONTPELLIER→

Olargues

22 23 24

1

Roquebrun

Pézenas

N9

20

A9

N112

Cessenon-sur-Orb

A75

N100

View across the Orb valley vineyards to the Gorges d'Héric (see Walk 12)

INTRODUCTION

You are walking under a clear blue sky; the light is sharp, the sun warm on your back, the air scented with rosemary, heather and broom. The silence is broken only by the humming of the bees. In the far distance, the waters of the Mediterranean glint in the sunlight, and the peaks of the Pyrenees shimmer above the heat haze rising from the valleys. Down below, on the plain, miles and miles of vineyards stretch to east and west, reminding you of the dinner you have booked at that very reasonable little restaurant. Welcome to the Languedoc!

The High Languedoc mountains lie to the west of the Cévennes, in the deep south of France. Sparsely populated and relatively little-known outside the area, they offer wonderful scenery, excellent walking at all levels and glimpses of an older way of life for which many of us yearn. It is rare that you see another human being on the trail except on busy holiday weekends, but if you do meet a local, you may find your GCSE French of little use! The accent is strong and lilting, a perfect accompaniment to the sunny, carefree climate. 'Pain' is pronounced 'peng' and 'vin' is 'veng' – so good luck (there is a short glossary at the back of the book to help you)!

This book aims to provide both the serious hiker and the gentle Sunday walker with opportunities to explore the Languedoc mountains and to enjoy the many variations of scenery, vegetation and geology. It concentrates particularly on those mountains which are situated between the towns of Béziers (south), Clermont l'Hérault (east), Saint-Pons (west) and La Salvetat (north), though some of the later walks go slightly beyond these boundaries.

The largest section of the High Languedoc mountains is the Espinouse massif. It is made up of three summits – Espinouse, Somail and Caroux – all just over 1000m high. Many of its ridges act as the watershed between the Atlantic and the Mediterranean, and because it forms a natural and geographical barrier it has been seen as something of a frontier throughout the history of the Languedoc region. Many invaders – Romans, Visigoths, Franks and others – have been limited in their progress by these heights.

From Neolithic times (3000BC) the broad ridges of the Espinouse were used by shepherds taking their flocks to new pastures, and there were numerous trading routes linking other provinces with the Mediterranean. Until the beginning of the 20th century, the agricultural economy was dominated by the production of chestnuts, and a large population invented many and varied ways of using them. Also, a lot of mining and charcoal burning took place on these mountainsides, and this activity was greatly responsible, along with sheep droving, for the establishment of so many of the paths described in this book. However, industrialisation, along with the effects of the two world wars, led to a huge exodus from the mountains. People flocked to the cities, leaving behind a large network of paths and drove roads which, with a gradual increase in leisure time, began to be used by city-dwellers for recreation.

Caroux is probably the best-known part of the Espinouse massif. Nicknamed 'Mountain of Light' because of the brightness of its rock faces, it soon became famous in the region as a hiking area; old paths were restored and waymarked, while new trails were opened by the Club Alpin Français. Many of these trails offer an invigorating challenge to the experienced walker. The summit plateaux of Somail and Espinouse are heavily wooded and offer less strenuous but very pleasant exercise.

To the south and east stretch a long line of foothills – the Avant-Monts, the Monts d'Orb, the hills of the Salagou valley, the Escandorgue – mostly covered thickly with evergreen oak and all providing delightful, secluded walking with fine views of the Espinouse massif, the Mediterranean plain or the Lac du Salagou. Many of the tracks are broad, used by farm and forestry vehicles; others, especially along the ridges, are very narrow, often used in the winter by hunters flushing out wild boar.

The variety of countryside is thrilling. To the north are the high *causses*, limestone plateaux with extraordinarily tortured rock formations. This is sheep country: windy, stark and mysterious, and very chilly in winter. Vast flocks of large, lean sheep, most unlike the cuddly Cotswold variety, roam these plateaux in the spring and summer, still often guided by lonely shepherds in the traditional beret of the region.

Drop down a little into the *hauts-cantons* above Bédarieux, and the hills are heavily wooded with oak, beech, pine and chestnut. Meadows are green and herds of cattle can be seen enjoying the lush grass. There are also a large number of goat farms, some run by refugees from the 'peace and love' days of the late 1960s, producing excellent round cheeses called *pelardons*. A wonderful sight, when in blossom in April, is the largest cherry orchard in Europe, situated on the plateau above Bédarieux (see Walk 21).

Once south of Bédarieux you are down on the Mediterranean plain and travelling through vineyards which are now among the finest in Europe. As little as 20 years ago, Languedoc wines were produced in huge quantities from poor grape varieties, and it is fair to say that most of them were dreadful. Fierce competition from Spain, Italy and the New World, combined with a 30% drop in home consumption of cheap table wines, forced the winemakers of the Languedoc to rethink their approach. Since the late 1980s they have been pursuing a policy of 'quality, not quantity', and wonderful wines can be found, not surprisingly, for the climate is ideal and the soil excellent. Try the reds of the Coteaux du Languedoc, Faugères and Saint-Chinian, and the rosé of Cabrières; enjoy the exquisite sweetness of Muscat – wonderful with Christmas pudding! But don't mix alcohol with the midday sun – not if you want to walk afterwards!

Further east, towards Clermont l'Hérault, there is the astonishing limestone chaos of the Cirque de Mourèze with, close by, the gritty red soil surrounding the Lac du Salagou. The area is a geologist's heaven.

CLIMATE, GEOLOGY, FLORA AND FAUNA

The heights of Espinouse and Somail act as the watershed between the Atlantic and the Mediterranean, and Caroux is situated entirely on the Mediterranean side of the watershed. As a result, the whole area is characterised by climatic instability and by a large number of microclimates. Summers are generally very warm with plenty of sunshine, while winter can bring strong winds, mist and snow to the tops. The end of summer is often punctuated by violent storms which dash against the hills and bring much needed water to the dried-up riverbeds.

The excesses of the climate have helped to create a rich and

A variety of Campanula

varied geology in the region. It is possible to find virtually any type of terrain or rock – basalt, volcanic lava, clay, limestone, schist, granite, gneiss – within a few square kilometres.

Vegetation, too, has had to adapt to climatic variations and is itself very rich and varied, with many species surviving at the limit of their natural area of growth. The tree cover is mainly evergreen oak, beech and chestnut, but this is somewhat masked on Somail and Espinouse by the generalised planting of pines. Along streams can be found ash, willow, poplar and walnut, hawthorn and large fern. At certain levels, and depending on soil acidity, Montpellier maples and arbutus, holly and cistus can be seen amongst the evergreen oak. Higher in the beech woods there is holly, laurel and yew, while some sphagnum peat can be seen up on the plateaux. In large areas of high plateau walkers can enjoy extensive covering of heather, wild thyme, broom and fern. Lack of pollution has encouraged the growth of moss and lichen.

Many of the animals and birds found in the Espinouse are similarly living at the limit of their normal geographical spread. Amongst the birds that can be seen are tits, warblers, Bonelli eagles, buzzards, falcons and eagle owls. You are likely to spot the occasional harmless grass snake, along with lizards, geckos, adders and salamanders; in the streams there are trout, while the Lac du Salagou is famous for its carp. Watch out for wild boar, squirrels, dormice, voles, hares and mouflon (a type of mountain goat introduced to the region from Corsica in the late 1950s; there are now over 1000 animals on the Espinouse).

GETTING THERE

By Car: It is always a shame to rush a journey through France, but if your time is short the motorway system is now very good. Try not to travel on weekends in July and August, as you will have half the population of Europe travelling with you.

From Calais, you can avoid Paris by going to Reims and on to Dijon and Lyon. There is now a ring-road round Lyon to make the journey quicker. The Rhône valley motorway divides north of Orange: take the A9 westwards, past Nîmes and Montpellier.

However, this is a busy route with expensive tolls. Far more pleasant is the new A75 which you pick up at Clermont Ferrand, having taken the A10 from Paris to Orléans and the A71 from Orléans to Clermont. Not only is the countryside spectacular from here to the south – there are no tolls beyond Clermont Ferrand.

By train: There is a TGV route from Lille or Paris to Montpellier, from where there are regular trains to Béziers. From Béziers there is a service to Bédarieux.

By air: British Airways run a twice-daily service from Gatwick to Montpellier, and Ryanair fly from Stansted to Carcassonne. From both these French airports, the High Languedoc mountains are about 90 minutes away. A hire car is strongly recommended.

WHERE TO STAY

If you have decided that walking in this area is to be the central feature of your holiday, then it would be useful to pick your accommodation somewhere near the D908 between Clermont l'Hérault and the village of Olargues, west of Lamalou les Bains. For hotels, your best bet is Lamalou. The broadest range of holiday-cottage accommodation is to be found in the *Gîtes de France* brochure for the Hérault area. Contact details are:

Gîtes de France Hérault, Maison du Tourisme, BP 3070, 34034 MONTPELLIER CEDEX 1. Tel: 00 33 4 67 67 71 62. e-mail: contact@gites-de-france-herault.asso.fr

There are camp-sites at Les Aires, near Lamalou, and at Bédarieux, Lamalou, Lac du Salagou, Laurens, Roquebrun, Mons la Trivalle and Olargues. For further information, contact local tourist offices:

	Tel	Address
Bédarieux	04 67 95 08 79	place Herbes, 34600 BEDARIEUX
Lamalou les Bains	04 67 95 70 91	2 av. Menard, 34240 LAMALOU LES BAINS
Octon (Salagou)	04 67 96 22 79	Le Village, 34800 OCTON
Olargues	04 67 97 71 26	av. de la Gare, 34390 OLARGUES
Pézenas	04 67 98 36 40	1 place Gambetta, 34120 PEZENAS
Roquebrun	04 67 89 79 97	Le Village, 34460 ROQUEBRUN
St Gervais sur Mare	04 67 23 68 88	Rue Pont, 34610 ST GERVAIS SUR MARE
St Guilhem le Désert	04 67 57 44 33	2 rue Font du Portal, 34150 ST GUILHEM LE D.

There are also:
- **Refuges** at Mons-la-Trivalle (Le Verdier Bas), Lafage (Rosis), Font-Salesse, Nostre Seigne, Les Bourdils, Le Crouzet, Campblanc. These are very basic mountain huts – do not expect more than a roof over your head.
- *Gîtes* at Combes, La Pomarède (St Martin de l'Arçon), Les Clèdes (Castanet-le-Haut) and Las Coumaires (Riols). There is also a very nice *ferme auberge* at Douch which offers lodging and an evening meal, reservation only, tel. 04 67 95 21 41.

WHAT TO SEE

There is the possibility that you will not want to spend every day of your holiday walking, and as far as general tourism is concerned the Languedoc is hard to beat. If you are desperate to join the hordes, there are miles of sandy beaches. Try Sérignan, which is a bit quieter than the more built-up Valras. There are many historic towns and villages to visit, some stunning countryside and, of course, all those wines to be tasted! A few places and suggested itineraries are given below.

- Exploration by car of the north side of **Caroux and Espinouse**. Follow miles of minor roads through beautiful countryside to Fraisse sur Agoût, La Salvetat and on up to the lakes of Laouzas and Raviège.
- **Lac du Salagou**: Swim, canoe or windsurf on the lake, cycle round it, visit nearby Mourèze and the *caveau* at Cabrières.
- **Pézenas**: a delightful town with a lovely main street and old

The church in the lovely old village of Mourèze, near Lac du Salagou (Walks 25 and 26)

quarter, the latter full, in summer, of interesting little shops. Worth visiting on a Saturday morning for the market.

• **Carcassonne**: this historic walled city is very impressive, but busy in the summer. In August there is a spectacular mediaeval pageant.

• **Cirque de Navacelles, Gorges de l'Hérault, Grotte des Demoiselles:** A geographer's day out! The cirque is a huge bowl carved out by the river, with a village sitting on a mound at the bottom. The Hérault river gorge is a must for lovers of tortured limestone. The *grotte* is a huge series of limestone caves with astonishing stalagmites and stalactites. One of the caverns is 52m high.

• **St Guilhem le Désert, Grotte de Clamouse:** With its wonderful abbey, St Guilhem is an important stop on one of the trails leading to St Jacques de Compostelle. The village square boasts the biggest plane tree in France. The *grotte* is another winner.

• **Sète**: The town centre sits astride a series of canals used by the port's fishing fleet. A very colourful place full of excellent seafood restaurants. Go up to the top of the Mont St Clair for a sweeping view across the bay to the Pyrenees. In late August, a form of water-borne jousting – les Joutes – takes place on the central canal; local teams row towards each other at great speed, the aim being to knock the opposing team's lance-bearer into the water. Visit the villages of Bouzigues and Mèze on the other side of the Etang (Lagoon) de Thau, the heart of the local oyster industry.

- **Roquebrun**: renowned for its microclimate, Roquebrun is nicknamed 'Petit Nice'. On the banks of the River Orb, the village is stunningly beautiful, best seen from the opposite bank, where a shingle beach is created each year. In February, the village holds a Mimosa Festival. Visit the Mediterranean Garden on the hillside above the village.

- **Béziers**: a very pleasant main square with some interesting side-streets. Worth going on Friday for the flower market. A large market hall is excellent for fish, fruit and vegetables, meat, cheeses, olives and spices. The Canal du Midi passes just to the south of the town. In mid-August, Béziers holds its *féria*, a riot of bullfighting, paella eating, sangria drinking, flamenco dancing and feeling rather ill!

- **Montpellier**: one of the fastest-developing cities in France, it has a wonderful Old Town full of chic boutiques and bistros. The main square, the Place de la Comédie, is the place to sit and people-watch; though, of course, walkers are far too serious-minded to do that sort of thing!

FOOD, MARKETS AND MONEY

There is nothing like wandering round a provincial French market if you want to experience the flavour of local life. Try Bédarieux (Monday mornings), Pézenas (Saturdays) and the market halls in Béziers, Sète, Montpellier and Lamalou.

If you wish to change money or increase your supply, there is a good selection of banks and cashpoints in all the local towns. Visa, Mastercard, Cirrus, and the like are all widely accepted, but it is common for English credit cards to be 'blocked' after one trans-action – be warned!

Note that France switches to the Euro on 1st January 2002.

WEATHER, CLOTHING AND EQUIPMENT

As with any mountainous area, the weather here can change quite quickly, but generally you can see the change coming from some distance away. The wind plays an important part in weather lore locally – there are 13 named winds – and you will soon hear about the *vent du Nord*, which brings clear skies, the *marin*, which brings thick rain clouds up from the sea, and the *Tramontane*, which blows mightily across from the northwest. In July and August, midday temperatures are very high, and you would be unwise to walk on exposed south-facing trails at this time.

What to wear? In the summer months it is likely that all you will need is a tee-shirt, shorts and light-weight walking boots. However, always have a showerproof coat in your rucksack, and take sun cream/block, sunglasses and a sunhat. Make sure your boots have good soles, as some of the paths are stony. Start early in the morning to avoid the hottest part of the day.

At other times of the year the weather can confound you. On many occasions it is possible to walk in a tee-shirt and shorts, but the warmth can not be guaranteed to last all day. Always have waterproof, windproof clothing, gloves and a hat available. Light-weight boots will still be more than adequate.

At all times of year it is advisable to take with you:
- map and compass (and know how to use them)
- plenty of water, at least a litre per person
- snacks/food
- whistle
- torch
- good first-aid kit.

In case of accident phone 18. This will connect you to an operation centre which will organise rescue or medical support. You are advised to have a valid E111 form to cover medical expenses, and accident insurance that covers evacuation from the mountains.

MAPS

Use the IGN Series 1:25,000, available at bookshops in the area. Also very useful is the map *Caroux et Bord Oriental de l'Espinouse*, by David Mazet, which shows all the mountain paths and peaks in much greater detail. For touring, the IGN 1:100,000 Béziers/Montpellier map is excellent.

USING THIS GUIDE

All the walks described are circular routes. In addition to a map of the whole area, there are two maps showing the start/end point for each route (see pages 8–11). Each walk is accompanied by a sketch map of the route, and the main features are emboldened in the text.

Each walk is labelled with a letter – **A, B or C**. These correspond to the following categories.

- **A** – steady path, no technical problems, no difficult ascents.
- **B** – More difficult due to either length of walk or steep ascents.
- **C** – Very demanding walk with steep ascents, exposed rock faces, possibly some scrambling. The path may be covered in loose stone.

Some walks come mainly within one category, but have a short section which is more demanding. This is signalled by, for example, 'B/C'.

HUNTING

Hunting plays a big part in the life of many local people. Of particular importance is the wild boar hunt, which occurs for five months of every year – normally end of August to end of January – on Wednesdays, Saturdays and Sundays. Hare and mouflon are also hunted.

If you find yourself in the middle of a 'beat', keep to the path and seek the advice of one of the hunters. Wear bright colours – red or orange, for example. The boar themselves are less dangerous than the hunters; they will generally shy away from humans unless their young are threatened – their wariness is well-advised, as *civet de sanglier* is often to be found in local restaurants!

RECOMMENDATIONS

Nature is very fragile in this area and often falls victim to fire at times of drought or high wind. Please therefore heed the following:

- Do not camp outside designated areas.
- Do not leave any rubbish behind.
- Do not stray from the path.
- Do not walk through crops or pick wild flowers.
- Do not disturb flocks of sheep or herds of cattle.
- Never light a fire or throw away a lighted cigarette.

Walk 1 – Around Roquebrun

Distance:	16km
Time:	5 hours
Total ascent:	450m
Grade:	B
Start point:	esplanade, Roquebrun
Maps:	IGN 2544 est (Murviel) and
	2544 ouest (St Chinian)

The village of Roquebrun is a gem. Situated in the heart of the beautiful Orb valley, with the river at its feet, it is a natural gateway to the High Languedoc Nature Park. Its lovely old buildings rise harmoniously up the hillside, and its position in the shelter of the hills gives it a very special microclimate. Known as the 'Little Nice', the village is home to many orange and lemon trees, and in late January/early February huge banks of mimosa provide a riot of colour. There is a mimosa festival in mid-February, with street processions, folk-dancing and general mayhem.

This walk takes you across exposed slopes and shady woodland into the isolated hills behind the village and provides excellent views in all directions – Caroux and Espinouse to the north, the Pyrenees and the sea to the south. A particular highlight is the visit to the isolated chapel of St Etienne, from which the view is sublime. If you do this walk in summer, an early start is recommended; the first part is south-facing and becomes very hot by midday.

How to get there   From Bedarieux take the D908 past Lamalou. Soon after Colombières, turn left on to the D14, the Orb valley road. On entering Roquebrun, go to the heart of the village and park on the esplanade near the restaurant Le Petit Nice (worth a visit after-wards for its wild boar cooked in red wine).

The route   From the esplanade walk along the road, in the direction of Vieussan; near the wine co-operative turn right up the Chemin des Olivettes, then left into the Chemin de la Garenne and right into the Chemin du Garrigas. At a fork by a telegraph pole, go right, following blue and yellow waymarks along a delightful path which winds up the hillside above the river and the village. (The blue and yellow marks signify two routes which stay together for the first

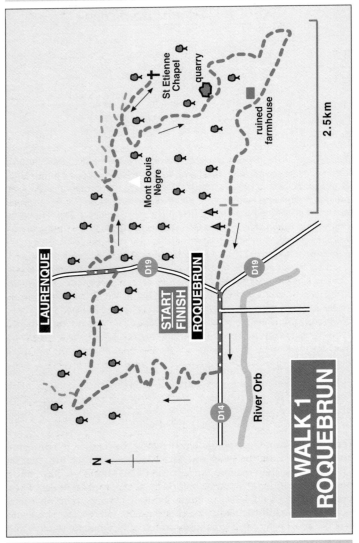

LAURENQUE

ROQUEBRUN

St Etienne Chapel

quarry

ruined farmhouse

Mont Bouis Nègre

2.5km

D19

D19

D14

River Orb

START FINISH

ROQUEBRUN

N

WALK 1
ROQUEBRUN

part of the walk; you will then follow the blue route to where it rejoins the yellow later on.)

There are lovely views across the vineyards and wooded hillsides. On a clear morning, Mont Canigou and other Pyrenean peaks stand out to the southwest, and the Mediterranean is visible to the south.

Eventually, pass through a short section of dry-stone wall and go past a ruined stone barn. The track now contours through oak trees and reveals, to your right, the wild, wooded valley through which you will soon walk, with the hamlet of Laurenque at the far end. A well-marked meander through the trees brings you to a clearing (barrier on the left); turn right along a broad track and after some 200m come to a clearing, often used as a meeting-place for hunters. Here, abandon the yellow waymarks and follow the blue, half-right across the clearing. The path drops down, soon passing a stone ruin. Cross a stream and follow its line down to the valley floor; cross it again and turn right alongside a stone wall. Turn left after some stone steps and come up to the road (D19 E1 to Laurenque).

Here, you have a choice; if you've had enough, turn right and walk back down the road to Roquebrun. Otherwise, our route takes us left along the road. After some 500m a concrete drive ascends to the right, by a telegraph pole. Follow it up for about 150m, then look for a narrow path going off to the right into the trees.

A long haul up the side of **Bouis Nègre** will show you how fit you are. You will eventually emerge onto a bend in a wide forest road. Ignoring yellow waymarks, look immediately right for a narrow path marked in blue. The climb up this path is equally long and even steeper, but just when you think you are completely exhausted, it arrives at a small clearing. Carry straight on and descend through trees to a clearing. Here starts your reward for all the slog – a magnificent view opens up of the Mediterranean plain, with the sea sparkling beyond. In the foreground are two conical hills; the Hermitage de St Etienne, an ancient chapel, is at the top of the nearest one and is your next target.

The track veers left and descends. Shortly, look east to see in the distance the pointed summit of the Pic de Vissou above Cabrières and, to its left, the Mont Liausson. Behind is the mass of the Pic St Loup, north of Montpellier. Off-track to the left, by an electricity line, you can see across to the Espinouse massif.

The elegant bridge over the River Orb at Roquebrun, one of the lovliest villages in the Languedoc

Go along a cart track through broom, then through an oak wood to reach a junction of paths. Carry straight on, following yellow waymarks as well as the blue. Passing a house on your right, come to a right-hand hairpin bend. Do not go round the bend, but follow the unmarked track which goes straight on through trees. At a clearing some 200m on, leave the main track and head 90 degrees right up a narrow unmarked path which climbs steadily. Shortly, reach the **chapel** and take in the view.

Nearly all the elements which make this area so special can be seen from here: Caroux, Espinouse, the foothills of the Cévennes, the plain, the sea with Sète and Agde clearly visible , the Pyrenees, the Orb valley and the villages (St Nazaire in the foreground, Autignac, Laurens and Magalas further east). The St Etienne chapel, open to the public, and is a delightful, vaulted structure, simply furnished; you will see that the tradition is to leave your name carved on a slate inside.

Retrace your steps to the hairpin bend and descend past an old house. The broad track takes you on past a marble **quarry**; as you pass under the face of the quarry, see the hermitage on the hill-top above. Some 400m after the quarry, on a col, look for a right-hand path which descends through trees (blue/yellow waymarks). The path is lined with *arbousier*, the strawberry tree, which in November is covered with cream-coloured flowers and bright red and orange fruits at the same time. The fruit is edible if you are desperate!

Soon, come through some vineyards, passing a ruined farmhouse on your right. At a junction go straight on, keeping a stand of pines on your right. At the top of the rise, pass the local archery club on your left and shortly see the village of **Roquebrun**, with its elegant bridge, ahead. Descend to the village and back to your car.

Walk 2 – La Forêt des Ecrivains Combattants

Distance:	6.6 km
Time:	2h30
Total ascent:	250m
Grade:	A/B
Start point:	Combes
Map:	IGN 2543 ouest (St Gervais)

High on the eastern slopes of Caroux, close to the Gorges de Madale, the Forêt des Ecrivains Combattants was planted in memory of French writers who died in combat, and the many paths leading through it are named after them. The walk is very varied: the mountain village of Combes is a delightful starting point, then plantations of chestnut forest give way to the pinewoods of the Forest. Eventually, the walker comes out onto the open ridge above the Gorges de Madale, with stupendous views down into the gorge and across to the Mediterranean coast. Though there is some uphill work, this is not a strenuous walk and is therefore a good introduction to the area. For a special treat at the end of the walk, book in to the Auberge de Combes, which provides clean, simple accommodation for hikers and serves large portions of excellent food, particularly locally hunted game, at very affordable prices (tel. 04 67 95 66 55).

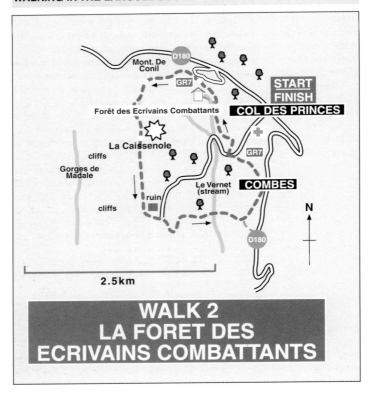

Forêt des Ecrivains Combattants

COL DES PRINCES

START
FINISH

COMBES

La Caissenole

Gorges de Madale

cliffs

cliffs

ruin

Le Vernet (stream)

Mont. De Conil

GR7

GR7

D180

D180

N

2.5km

WALK 2
LA FORET DES
ECRIVAINS COMBATTANTS

How to get there From Lamalou les Bains, take the D908 to Le Poujol sur Orb and, in the village, look for a turn to the right (D180), signed 'Combes/Rosis'. Follow this road up to **Combes** and park at the entrance to the village.

The route Walk along the road through the village. Immediately opposite the last house, turn sharp left up a narrow road, waymarked in red and white (this is the **GR7**, a long-distance path, which you will follow up to the mountain top). The road leads above the village and, opposite the last dwelling, look for a path going off uphill to the right (red/white waymarks). This is a beautifully laid stone track through the chestnut and oak trees – a joy to walk. Take a sharp left-hand bend by a bay tree and continue between dry-stone walls to reach a narrow road. Turn left and walk along the road for some 200m to a sign reading 'Parcours Sportif' ('Fitness Trail'). Stay on the road here as it bears right, then right again at the next fork, followed by a further sharp right. Tarmac now gives way to a broad dirt track, which swings left and soon brings you to a sign announcing entry into the forest area. You will start to see small stone monuments, each bearing the name of a writer, the first of whom is a certain Lucien Graux. After about 100m, bear right onto a grassy track that leads to a green and white stone **roundabout** in a clearing. Go across the roundabout and left up the 'Chemin Louis Pergaud', then fork half-right up a grassy track between tall pines. A short slog brings you up to a clearing with a **roundabout** in the middle (Rond-point Maurice Bourdet, with a tree in the middle of the roundabout). From here, there are extensive views to the north and down to the sea.

Now, go down a grassy track to the right of a monument to Lt.-Col. De Malleray and descend southwest to a junction (large cairn). Leave the GR7 to the right and go straight on to a **roundabout** (A. Bertrand); left of the marker-post, head south on a narrow path that climbs back to the edge of the forest, giving lovely open views across to the gorge and village of Madale. On reaching another small roundabout (Belvédère P. Chanlaine), take a small path to the right for about 30m to reach the summit of **La Caissenole**, from which you get a magnificent view of the Mediterranean coastline and surrounding hills.

Carry on south-southwest along a narrow ridge path to the next small summit some 50m away, then drop down, half-left, between rocks and through oak trees to a wide col. The path now goes straight and slightly downhill, and you can soon see a line of cairns ahead. (It is well worth going off-route at this point to scramble around the rocks by the highest cairn. The view down into the Gorges de Madale is quite vertiginous. Then retrace your steps.) However, at the obvious low point in the path, you must now look carefully for a path going off to the left, just past a **ruined sheepfold** (blue triangular waymarks, which you will now follow all the way back to Combes). Follow this down to a dirt road about 300m away, passing two more ruined stone buildings on the way. Turn right on to the dirt road and descend some 300m south, then turn sharply northeast, with the roofs of the hamlet of Le Vernet below, before swinging east and crossing the Vernet stream by a concrete ramp. Carry on until you come to a left-hand bend. Do not continue on the broad track, but instead look for a slightly narrower, initially grassy track going off sharply to the left and gently uphill. This leads after about 100m to a tennis court and tiny soccer pitch. Take a narrow path above the left-hand side of the pitch and follow it gently downhill to come out on to the road in the centre of **Combes** with, if you have timed it right, the rich aromas of roasting game wafting up to you from the restaurant kitchens! Go on, treat yourself!

Walk 3 – Les Gorges de Madale

Distance:	11.6km
Time:	4h30
Total ascent:	580m
Grade:	B/C
Start point:	Sevirac
Map:	IGN 2543 ouest (St Gervais)

A fascinating and quite strenuous walk up the southeastern slope of Caroux, offering the isolated splendour of the Gorges de Madale. The gorge is quite narrow and enclosed, much less visited than the much larger Gorges de Colombières (Walk 4) and, as a result, has a much wilder feel to it. The walk takes you up through the woods to the magnificent Pilier du Bosc, a rock face 200m high much loved by local climbers, then on to the tiny hamlet of Madale before returning via the edge of the Forêt des Ecrivains Combattants (Walk 2) and down an easy ridge path. Take a compass.

How to get there Take the D908 from Bedarieux, and about 1km from Colombières take a right turn to Sevirac. Park about 200m from the farm there.

The route Walk north to the farm; go right behind the buildings and continue alongside vines, following the blue waymarks.

ROSIS

D180

MADALE

Forêt des Ecrivains
Combattants

GR7

N

COMBES

Pilier
du
Bosc

LE VERNET

WALK 3
LES GORGES
DE MADALE

gorge

combe

SEVIRAC
START
FINISH

D908

River Orb

2.5km

Descend left and go along a narrow ledge to cross a stream (Madale). A few metres further up, take the gorge path and climb northwards through a chestnut wood. The route takes you across some scree and then over some tilted rock-slabs before coming to a clearing in the oak trees where, until the beginning of the 20th century, charcoal burners used to work. Walk above the old stone shelter to reach a small promontory which overlooks the gorge. Climb to the left and head north through the trees along a path with cairns; cross a rock-fall and negotiate a fairly exposed ledge. Next come some more tilted slabs of rock, then you descend to the north across some scree. At a low point in the path, a cairn marks the access to the **Pilier du Bosc**, a high rock on which many climbers practise.

Climb to the left over a series of slabs, then traverse through chestnut trees and heather. A short descent through rocks brings you to the stream. Follow it for a while, then leave the stream bed up a steep earth track. Follow the path, staying in the chestnut trees and ignoring a north-bound path through the heather and broom. A series of bends brings you up to an old sheepfold alongside a cart-track. Follow this track north to the hamlet of **Madale**. Walk through the hamlet and, after about 80m, turn right (southeast) off the road onto a sheep-drovers' track with red/white waymarks (these denote you are on a long-distance path, the GR7). Go down to the stream, and take advantage of this fine spot for a picnic!

Continue along the left bank, climbing up to the ridge and on to the edge of the forest (Forêt des Ecrivains Combattants), enjoying views of the mountains to the north. At a junction of forestry roads leave the GR7 and go right, soon reaching a roundabout (A. Bertrand). Left of the marker-post, head south on a path which climbs back to the edge of the forest. Walk about 30m past the Belvédère P. Chanlaine, to the right, and reach the summit of La Caissenole, from which you get a magnificent view of the Mediterranean coastline.

Go south-southwest along a narrow ridge path which climbs once before dropping down between rocks to a wide col amongst oak trees and beside a ruined sheepfold (red waymarks). At a low point in the path, leave the red waymarks and descend left to a dirt road about 300m away. Descend to the right (south) through chestnut trees; at the first intersection bear left along a dirt road and

Roquebrun, on the banks of the River Orb (Walk 1)

The Gorges d'Héric viewed from the Col de l'Airole (Walks 8 & 9)

From the viewing platform on Mont Caroux (Walk 10)

Caroux from the old hillside village of Vieussan

past a spring (source du Pradet). Soon you will reach the hamlet of
Le Vernet. Climb to the right of a small wash-house and traverse
the village. As you reach the last houses, descend left along a dirt
road, and at the first fork go straight on, then left to reach the road
(D180E). Leave the road immediately, taking a right turn on to an
obvious path (south). When the cement comes to an end, continue
left for 100m and then right through the vines.

Follow the contours of a broad combe to a plateau. To the left
drop to the south-west on a path which brings you to a wide lane.
Follow this right, above some vineyards and after a short descent,
return to the point of departure.

Walk 4 – Les Gorges de Colombières

Distance:	10.7km
Time:	4 hours
Total ascent:	630m
Grade:	B
Start point:	Colombières-sur-Orb
Map:	IGN 2543 ouest (St Gervais)

*The Gorges de Colombières walk is one of the most exciting outings on the
eastern end of Mont Caroux, providing spectacular views down into the
gorge and, from the top, a huge panorama of the coastal plain and the
Pyrenees. The climb from Colombières up through woodland to the highest
point involves a change in altitude of some 600m, most of it quite steady,
but take plenty of water and a picnic. If you feel like roughing it, the Refuge
of Lafage is at the top of the walk. There is a restaurant in the recently
renovated farmhouse of Les Avels (see map). The return along the western
side of La Cabrière is very open at the top and provides a magnificent view
to the south from near the Roc de Bretouyre. If you are very quiet, you may
see a family of mountain goats before you drop back down into woodland.*

How to get there Reach the village of Colombières-sur-Orb by the
D908 from Bédarieux. Immediately after a bridge over a stream,
turn right to find a car park next to a school.

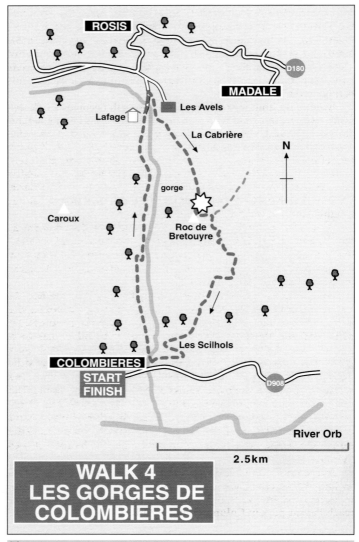

ROSIS

MADALE

D180

Les Avels

Lafage

La Cabrière

N

gorge

Caroux

Roc de
Bretouyre

Les Scilhols

COLOMBIERES
START
FINISH

D908

River Orb

2.5km

WALK 4
LES GORGES DE
COLOMBIERES

The route   Walk back towards the bridge and, just after a small water-treatment plant, find a stone staircase on the right (red waymark). Go up quite steeply and join a very obvious track. From here, keep on this track, taking care to follow the waymarks (now blue). As you go higher and enter chestnut forest, the track often twists and turns, so if you don't see an obvious blue mark, look behind and above you!

Eventually, after about 90 minutes, the path becomes a balcony walk above the gorge and you see ahead of you the buildings of the **Refuge of Lafage**, where walkers may seek shelter overnight. Contact the Club Alpin Français for details (04 67 28 09 68). Beyond the refuge a small tarmac road takes you across the stream. A few metres further on, leave the road to follow a right-hand path which takes you past the **ferme des Avels**, a lovely example of a local farm building, now restored as a restaurant. You are now heading roughly south through the heather and broom.

At a fork, ignore the Piste de la Buffe and take the other track, the Piste de la Cabrière. Along this track, the view down into the gorge is superb. As you walk parallel to the gorge, look out for *mouflon* on the rocks – these are a Corsican species of wild goat, introduced into the area in the 1950s.

Soon you reach a promontory some 80m north of the Roc de Bretouyre, from where you have a **huge** view of the gorge, the surrounding cliffs and hillsides, and (on a clear day) the coastal plain and the Pyrenees. The path curves left and comes to a junction. Go right onto the Chemin des Fleysses, an old Roman route which winds its way down through oak and chestnut woods. At one of the bends, a cairn marks the start of another path, the Sentier de Saucani. Follow it across a stream and walk south. The track widens and leads to a bend which has been cemented. Carry straight on down an obvious track; this soon bends round to a stand of cherry trees. Here, pick up the old track again, lower down to the right, and walk westwards, soon reaching the hamlet of **Les Seilhols**.

In the tiny square, find a steep stone stairway which descends to the right between houses. This eventually brings you down to the main road (D908). Turn right, over the bridge and right again to reach the car park in **Colombières-sur-Orb**.

Walk 5 – Saint Martin de l'Arçon

Distance:	9km
Time:	4h30
Total ascent:	640m
Grade:	B/C
Start point:	St Martin de l'Arçon
Map:	IGN 2543 ouest (St Gervais)

St Martin de l'Arçon is a charming village, full of carefully renovated old houses and intriguing alley-ways, nestling part-way up the southern slopes of Mont Caroux. A number of trails depart from the village to explore the mountain, and this walk is a good introduction to them. It is a delightful path providing an interesting and varied walk across open ground and through woodland, with excellent views of the foothills and of the Orb valley. It is sheltered from the north wind, so is a good one to do even in winter, and particularly after rain, as it passes under the Torrent d'Albine, one of the finest waterfalls on Caroux. There are a couple of tricky sections to negotiate, one at the waterfall and another on the exciting Piste des Biterrois path, so do take care.

How to get there From Lamalou les Bains follow the D908 west through Le Poujol. After Colombières, watch for signs right to St Martin de l'Arçon. The road goes up about 1km. Park just outside the village.

The route Walk up the road into the village. Look for signs right to the Mas de Rouyre (blue triangular waymark) leading up a stone alley between houses. Soon pass the Mas de Rouyre on your left and come to a fork towards the top of the village. Abandon the triangular markings and bear right (blue-lined waymarks) past the last two houses to follow a path which rises gently to the east towards a squat water tower visible on the ridge ahead. Just before the water tower go left 90 degrees up a stone path and then up through oak and chestnut trees, gradually swinging northwards to reach the **Ribassounes ravine**. Cross the ravine by a stone footbridge and climb between two walls, turning steadily east and passing through chestnut and oak trees. Go left of a ruin then past another one to follow an open path above the hamlet of La

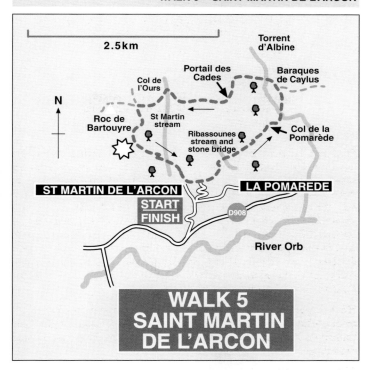

Pomarède. The path climbs gently to the **Col de la Pomarède**, a flat area on a ridge by a rocky outcrop. From here there is an excellent view of the Albine ravine and the wall of the Roque Rouge on the other side. It is worth diverting off the path to the east in order to find a seat on a rock and look up the entire fall of the stream (Albine) from the plateau to the base of the cliff.

From the col turn left (north), soon to cross over a chaos of rocks. The **Torrent d'Albine** soon comes into view, one of the loveliest waterfalls on Caroux. The path then bears right, down towards the waterfall, passing to the right of some huge rock slabs. An easy passage over some rocks leads to the foot of the waterfall, where you cross the stream.

Old stone barn in the mountain village of St Martin de l'Arçon

On the other side, go up a steep, narrow passage by the fall, soon leaving it and bearing right across some rock slabs. Then, coming back left above the slabs, find a broad path through trees, then a steep climb through ferns and chestnut trees to arrive at a junction with another path (Sentier de Garel, yellow waymarks). Turn left on to this path and head up through the trees to reach the ruins of two stone buildings, the **Baraques de Caylus**.

Here the path forks – continue left on the Sentier de Garel (yellow marks) and climb northwest, ignoring a blue-marked path to your right. Leave the chestnut wood and cross the Albine again. Head west through green oaks and, at the brow of a hill, come to a fork. Leave the yellow-marked path and follow the blue marks. You are now on the Piste des Biterrois (PDB). Cross the ravine (des Drayes), and on a balcony path heading south reach the base of a grassy couloir. Go up it to reach the **Portail des Cades**, a magnificent gap in the rock. Go through the gap, down through the trees and make a long traverse west to the eastern Col des Jonquilles. Climb down some rocks, then go up gently, through a rock-fall, to the western Col des Jonquilles.

Go down another rock-fall and walk westwards alongside the cliffs of the Arête de St Martin. Ignore the yellow-marked track on your left and carry on along the blue track through oak woods to a stream. Cross it, go steeply up, then wind down westwards to another stream (St Martin).

The path twists and turns south then climbs west through a gap; a last sharp rise brings you to the ridge at the **Col de l'Ours**. Going west, avoid a barrier of rock by climbing to the right; 100m further on, the Piste des Biterrois ends at a junction with another path, the Sentier des Gardes (red waymarks).

Follow this path and soon reach a fork (cairn); to the left of the cairn look for three steps which indicate the start of the Sentier de St Martin (red waymarks). Go down the steps and follow the path south through the oakwoods to a rocky promontory. Enjoy a view of the Orb valley then bear left (southeast) to cross an inclined slab of rock. Come to the edge of a chestnut wood; the path goes off to the right before coming back further down to go through the wood. Cross the stream and soon arrive back at the 'Mas plus haut', the highest house in St Martin.

Walk 6 – Circuit of the Caroux Plateau

Distance:	8km
Time:	6 hours
Total ascent:	650m
Grade:	C
Start point:	St Martin de l'Arçon
Map:	IGN 2543 ouest (St Gervais)

Another outing from Saint Martin de l'Arçon, providing a wonderful airy walk with excellent views into the heart of Caroux and across the foothills to the coast. As with Walk 5, the hiker comes to the foot of the magnificent waterfall known as the Torrent d'Albine. Another particular feature is the traverse of the Roque Rouge, an exposed, inclined slab high up above the valley. The path then goes up onto the open summit plateau of Caroux, crosses the Tourbière de la Lande, a large peat bog, and descends via the magnificent Sentier des Gardes, a path that gives superb views into the Gorges d'Héric.

How to get there From Lamalou les Bains follow the D908 west through Le Poujol. After Colombières, watch for signs right to St Martin de l'Arçon. The road goes up about 1km. Park just outside the village.

The route See Walk 5 for the route up to the ruins of the **Baraques de Caylus**. Just beyond the ruins turn right (blue waymarks), first through bushes then over rocky inclines, and climb steeply, changing direction (keep a careful eye on the waymarks) to reach a large cairn. The route now leads round the great slab of the **Roque Rouge**; some sections are quite narrow and exposed, but it is not technically difficult. Stay close to the trees if you don't like the edge! From here take in the breathtaking views down to the valley below and to the Tour Carrée, the remains of a mediaeval fortification above Colombières.

At the end of the passage, climb up a few metres and walk on to a junction with another path (red waymarks). Turn left onto this path, which within a few metres turns left, almost back on itself, then winds roughly northwards up the eastern side of the Roque Rouge, marked by small cairns. Eventually it reaches the plateau

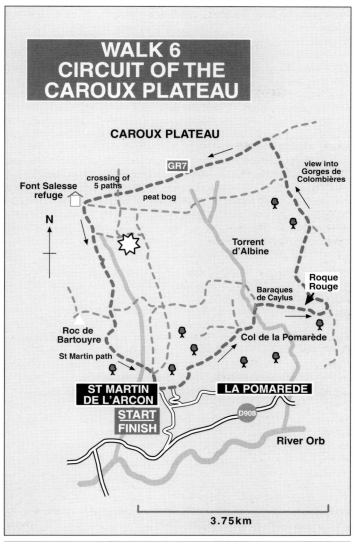

WALK 6
CIRCUIT OF THE
CAROUX PLATEAU

CAROUX PLATEAU

GR7

crossing of
5 paths

peat bog

view into
Gorges de
Colombières

Font Salesse
refuge

N

Torrent
d'Albine

Roque
Rouge

Baraques
de Caylus

Roc de
Bartouyre

Col de la Pomarède

St Martin path

ST MARTIN
DE L'ARCON

LA POMAREDE

START
FINISH

D908

River Orb

3.75km

and crosses a long stretch of heather. It is worth straying off to the rocks on the right to have a view down into the Gorges de Colombières (Walk 4) and the hill of La Cabrière (Walk 7) opposite.

Ignore all joining paths until you reach the junction with the GR7 long-distance path (red/white waymarks, large cairn). Turn left onto the GR7. The path widens into a track, but after about 1km you leave the track and go left down a track marked 'Tourbière [peat-bog] de la Lande', past the ruins of a stone building and walk on boards across the bog. Go on about 500m, eventually to arrive at a crossing of five paths. Take the path opposite, which leads directly to the **Refuge of Font Salesse** in 5 to 10 minutes.

With your back to the door of the Refuge, head straight through the trees, southwards (blue triangular waymark) down the Sentier des Gardes. Initially a broad forest track, the path narrows as it twists down the ridge, at first to the left of an imposing rocky outcrop. Before starting the descent, head into the rocks on the right for another breathtaking view, this time into the Gorges d'Héric (Walk 12).

The descent is a long series of hairpin bends with small cairns and faded red waymarks to guide you. Ignore all joining paths until you come to the junction with the **St Martin path** (large cairn and sign). From here the route is obvious. Drop down to the left and steeply through chestnut trees to cross a stream by a wooden footbridge. Arrive after about 40 minutes at **St Martin**.

Walk 7 – La Cabrière

Distance:	6.5 km
Time:	2 hours
Total ascent:	150m
Grade:	A
Start point:	near Rossis
Map:	IGN 2543 ouest (St Gervais)

La Cabrière is a hill divided from the eastern end of Mont Caroux by the dramatic Gorges de Colombières. This walk begins with a delightful, steady balcony walk (shared with Walk 4) below the summit, with stunning views into the gorge, down to the coast and along the valley of the River Orb. The second half explores the woodland above the Gorges de Madale before returning over the brow of La Cabrière.

How to get there On the D908 past Lamalou les Bains, come to Le Poujol. About three-quarters of the way through the village, turn

right (signed for Combes/Rosis). Start a long and spectacular climb up the mountain, through Combes (*auberge* has great food and a wonderful outdoor terrace), past the Clinique St Vital and on to Rosis. About 1.2km after Rosis, at a sharp right-hand bend, take a narrow road left (it may be signed for Lafage). Park immediately.

The route Walk down the narrow tarmac road, **not** the dirt road to the restaurant. On the left, some 60m before a stream, go left along a path (blue waymarks) which takes you past the **ferme des Avels**, a lovely example of a local farm building, now restored as a restaurant, the Relais du Montagnard. You are heading roughly south through the heather and broom. At a fork, ignore the Piste de la Buffe and take the other track, the Piste de la Cabrière. Along this track, the view down into the Gorge de Colombières is superb. As you walk parallel to the gorge, look out for *mouflon* on the rocks – these are a Corsican species of wild goat introduced into the area in the 1950s. Soon you reach a promontory from which you have a huge view of the gorge, the surrounding cliffs and hillsides and, on a clear day, the coastal plain and the Pyrenees.

The path curves left and comes to a junction. Ignore the **Chemin des Fleysses** which descends to your right and continue on the Sentier de Madale (rare yellow waymarks). The stony path curves eventually round to the north, descends steeply through chestnut woods and rises to a tarmac track by a small building which houses a spring. Continue on along the track (15–20mins) to **Madale**, to where the track becomes the road through the hamlet. Follow the road north out of the hamlet for about 100m, and at a left-hand bend turn left onto an obvious track with red/white markings (this is part of the GR7 long-distance footpath that traverses Caroux and Espinouse). The path is an old sheep-drovers' track, still in use.

Climb gently through heather and broom and make a long traverse of the north slope of La Cabrière. On reaching a track suitable for vehicles, turn right, and walk 100m back to your car.

Walk 8 – Tour du Roc Noir

Distance:	7.6km
Time:	2h45
Total ascent:	520m
Grade:	B
Start point:	Douch
Map:	IGN 2543 ouest (St Gervais)

A superb, energetic walk partly open and partly through woodland to the north of Mont Caroux, exploring the villages of Douch and Héric, which give you an idea of the harshness and remoteness of rural life a century ago, and the valley of the Vialais, hemmed in by giant cliffs, including the soaring outcrop of the Roc Noir (watch out for deer and wild boar). Views of the Gorges d'Héric and the Pyrenees from above Douch are stunning. There is a gîte in Douch, La Jasse, where you can get lodging and a meal (reservation only, tel. 04 67 95 65 76).

How to get there On the D908 past Lamalou les Bains, come to Le Poujol. About three-quarters of the way through the village, turn right (signed for Combes/Rosis). Start a long and spectacular climb up the mountain, through Combes (the *auberge* is recommended for its food and wonderful outdoor terrace), past the Clinique St Vital and on to Rosis. About 2km after Rosis, fork left to Douch. Just before the village there is a car park, left.

The route Go up to the village. At a small square (there is a small stone hut housing a spring where you can fill your bottle), the path goes up between trees and a field (heading southwest), past a stand of broom, and soon reaches a col (**Col de l'Airole**). Enjoy the view of the Gorges d'Héric! Do not go straight on – you'll come back that way – but turn right towards some old sheepfolds and pick up blue waymarks.

Traverse a large combe and reach a col covered in heather. Turn right and head north into the valley of a stream (**Salis**). Cross the stream, turn southwest, then walk gradually northwest for 100m to arrive at another col (**Col du Salis**), where you find the junction with the Vialais path. Go left (red waymarks) and down (southeast) through beech woods and cross the Salis ravine. On the western

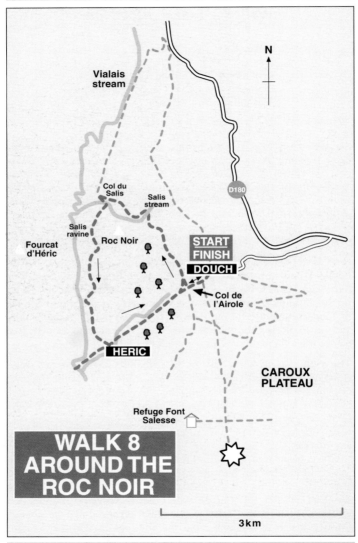

N

Vialais
stream

D180

Col du
Salis

Salis
stream

Salis
ravine

Roc Noir

Fourcat
d'Héric

START
FINISH
DOUCH

Col de
l'Airole

HERIC

CAROUX
PLATEAU

Refuge Font
Salesse

**WALK 8
AROUND THE
ROC NOIR**

3km

The church at Douch, on the approach to the Caroux plateau

slopes of the Roc Noir the path looks down on the stream (Le Vialais). Ignore a higher path (blue waymarks) and carry on, passing above an old sheepfold. Move away from the stream, heading south, and start to climb gently over the brow of a hill. Then go down until you reach the village of **Héric**.

The path back to Douch is well signed: it is part of the GR7 long-distance path. Just head northeast out of the village and keep going! The ascent takes about an hour and brings you back to the Col de l'Airole. From there, enjoy one more look at the view before heading down to **Douch**.

Walk 9 – Valley of the Vialais and the Montagne d'Aret

Distance:	10.4km
Time:	3h30
Total ascent:	450m
Grade:	B
Start point:	Douch
Map:	IGN 2543 ouest (St Gervais)

Starting from the same place as Walk 8, this is another delightful exploration of the valley of the Vialais, a favourite haunt for the mouflon, an imported Corsican mountain goat much loved in the area. This time, the walk heads north, dropping gradually down through woodland to the stream itself before turning away to climb up to the Col de l'Ourtigas. The return stretch, across the broad, treeless ridge of the Montagne d'Aret, rarely drops below 1000m, so views in all directions are stunning.

How to get there See Walk 8 for access to the hamlet of Douch. Just before the village there is a car park, left.

The route Go up to the village. At a small square the path goes up through the field (heading southwest), past a stand of broom, and soon reaches a col (**Col de l'Airole**). Enjoy the view of the Gorges d'Héric! Do not go straight on; turn right towards some old sheep-folds and pick up blue waymarks.

Traverse a large combe and reach a col covered in heather. Turn right and head north into the valley of a stream (Salis). Cross the stream, turn southwest, then walk gradually northwest for 100m to arrive at another col (**Col du Salis**), where you find the junction with the Vialais path. Go right (north) along the red-waymarked path and after about 15 minutes reach another col (Col du Mayne). Further on there is yet another col, east of the Roc Traucat.

Now heading northeast, the path drops into the woods and gradually approaches the Vialais stream, finally reaching it at a bridge (**Pont du Vialais**). Do not cross it, but go 20m backwards and find a path which climbs eastwards. At a fork go left up a good path

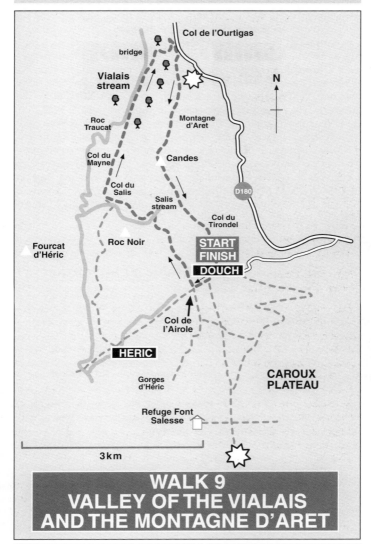

Col de l'Ourtigas

bridge

Vialais stream

N

Roc Traucat

Montagne d'Aret

Col du Mayne

Candes

Col du Salis

D180

Salis stream

Col du Tirondel

Fourcat d'Héric

Roc Noir

START FINISH

DOUCH

Col de l'Airole

HERIC

Gorges d'Héric

CAROUX PLATEAU

Refuge Font Salesse

3km

WALK 9
VALLEY OF THE VIALAIS
AND THE MONTAGNE D'ARET

which gently zig-zags up the hill. As it levels out, pass a picnic site and arrive at the road at the **Col de l'Ourtigas**.

To the right of the car park area, the path climbs steeply above the col on to the **Montagne d'Aret** – then, to the left, you reach a rocky promontory which gives you a broad view of the Montagne de Rosis and the mountains of the Orb valley. Carry on along the ridge, heading south, and reach a track which acts as a fire-belt. Follow this along the ridge, passing a cage used for capturing *mouflons*.

When the fire-belt ends, continue on a yellow-waymarked path, which drops into a combe before rising again to the summit of **Candes**, then continues on to a col (Tirondel). From there, abandon the yellow waymarks and climb towards the southeast, passing over a col and down to the left of some beech trees in which you can see the ruins of a sheepfold. From here, enjoy a splendid view of Douch and the north slopes of Caroux. Contnue along an old sheep-drovers' path to arrive at **Douch**.

Walk 10 – Caroux – Table d'Orientation

Distance:	6.5km
Time:	2 hours
Total ascent:	140m
Grade:	A
Start point:	Douch
Map:	IGN 2543 ouest (St Gervais)

An easy walk from Douch (see Walks 8 and 9) that takes you painlessly up to the broad Caroux plateau (over 1000m high) and across to the viewing platform on the southern face of the mountain. From here, there are fantastic views of the Pyrenees, coastal plain, Cevennes and Montagne Noire. Definitely one for a family picnic!

How to get there See Walk 8 for access to the hamlet of Douch. Just before the village there is a car park, left.

The route (See also alternative route below.) Go to the barrier at the far end of the car park and follow the wide track beyond – it zig-

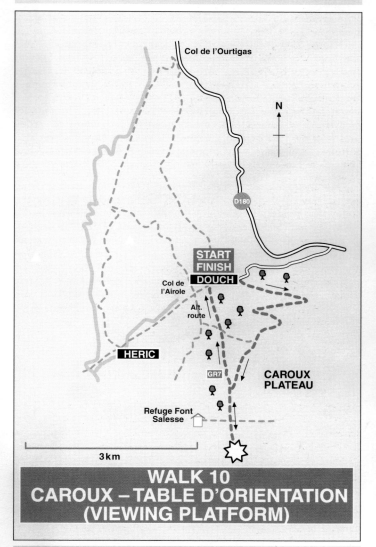

Col de l'Ourtigas

N

D180

START
FINISH
DOUCH

Col de
l'Airole

Alt.
route

HERIC

GR7

CAROUX
PLATEAU

Refuge Font
Salesse

3 km

WALK 10
CAROUX –TABLE D'ORIENTATION
(VIEWING PLATFORM)

zags steadily up the north slope of Caroux and arrives at a col. Continue westwards, passing a ruined sheepfold (Jasse d'Alingri), and come to a fork. Continue straight on, heading south. At a junction with the GR7 footpath, continue south through trees to reach a rocky promontory, where you will see a *table d'orientation* (viewing platform). On the platform is a ceramic table which names the features visible from this point.

To return, go back through the trees to the junction with the GR7 (red/white waymarks). This time, ignore the path you used earlier, and take the GR7 heading north back towards **Douch** (there is a little red/white sign, so you can't go wrong). The path crosses the plateau and descends steadily through beechwoods to the village.

For an alternative, and slightly more demanding, route go from the car park to the square in front of the village. From the square, follow the red/white marks of the GR7 between the trees and a field. The path soon opens up and reaches the **Col de l'Airole**, with its magnificent view down into the Gorges d'Héric. From the col, an unmarked path leads steeply up the slope to your left. At the top of the slope the path joins a wider track. Go left and soon come to a junction with the GR7 (red/white waymarks) on the plateau above Douch. Go right and follow this path to the viewing platform. You then have the choice of returning to **Douch** by the same route or by the main route described above.

Walk 11 – Circuit of La Gleizo

Distance:	6.4km
Time:	3 hours
Total ascent:	490m
Grade:	C
Start point:	Mons
Map:	IGN 2543 ouest (St Gervais)

An invigorating and, on the descent, quite demanding walk on the Gleizo massif, a mountain separated from Caroux by the astonishing Gorges d'Héric. Starting from the village of Mons/La Trivalle (café and a few shops), the upward trail takes you gently through woodland on the western slopes of the Gleizo massif (as with many other place names in the area, numerous spelling variations exist: Gleyzo, Gleyse, etc). The return brings you back over the higher part of the mountain, providing numerous opportunities to look across to the cliffs of the Gorges d'Héric as well as the Espinouse and the Jaur valley. Care is needed on a short but steep descent from the Col de Roujas.

How to get there Travelling from Lamalou les Bains on the D908, reach the Mons/La Trivalle turn-off. Turn right and follow the D14 E20 to Mons. Park opposite the church.

The route From the church climb northwards, through the village, to a fork by a metal cross and some allotments. Go right, up a steep cemented track, then take a stone alley to the right between two houses, following red and blue waymarks. Turn left after these houses to reach a stone path which in years gone by was the main route connecting Mons and Bardou. Follow this up the ravine, eventually crossing over the stream and ignoring a blue waymark to the right which leads up the ravine. Follow the winding path through chestnut and oak trees (waymarks are scarce at first but soon you see regular blue triangles and red lines). (Note that often on a slope the path is constructed *en calade* – with the stones placed edge up; this helps to prevent erosion during heavy storms.)

After a longish haul upwards the path flattens out and you begin to see extensive views of Espinouse, the Jaur valley and, to the south, the Pic de Naudech. Soon, come out of the trees and reach a rocky promontory from which to really enjoy those views. Then, back into the trees! Climb to the northwest and make a long balcony traverse through chestnut trees. As the path starts to climb again towards the **Col de la Maure** (or Molle), look carefully on your right for the start of the Gleizo path. **Take care here – this junction is not entirely obvious**. The path is marked by faded yellow marks on two trees, and there is a small cairn. Follow the yellow markings, mostly faint and painted on rocks. Look out for herds of deer and *mouflon*. Climb through the trees, soon heading southeast alongside the ridges. You are soon conscious that a huge view of the **Gorges d'Héric** is opening out to your left, and you will soon see, some 40m west of the path, a rocky platform from which to enjoy it.

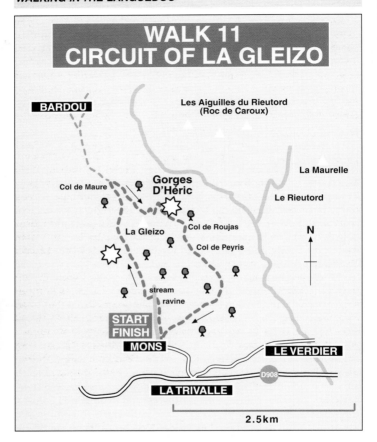

WALK 11
CIRCUIT OF LA GLEIZO

BARDOU

Les Aiguilles du Rieutord
(Roc de Caroux)

Col de Maure

Gorges
D'Héric

La Maurelle

Le Rieutord

La Gleizo

Col de Roujas

Col de Peyris

N

stream

ravine

START
FINISH

MONS

LE VERDIER

LA TRIVALLE

D908

2.5km

Immediately opposite is an enormous slab of rock which forms the highest and most breathtaking part of the gorge. The drop to the road below is quite vertiginous.

Back on the path, a short climb brings you over the Gleizo ridges, with the former view of the Espinouse and Jaur valley coming back into focus. Soon come to a large rock promontory with a cairn and a rusted sign. On a clear day you will see the sea to the south and the Pyrenees to the southwest. Retrace your steps a few metres from the cairn, pass to the right of a large oak bush, and go sharply uphill (northeast) before dropping down to the east, where a view of the Gorges d' Héric opens up again. Scramble over a few large rocks, then look immediately right to pick up the waymark. In front of you shortly is a very obvious col, the **Col de Roujas**. Head for a marker post, clearly visible on that col. You will surely be tempted to scramble up to the summit behind the marker post; the near 360 degree view is well worth the effort.

From the marker post red waymarks direct you north, down a steep and badly-eroded slope. **Take great care here!** The waymarking is a bit fitful but look for a large pine tree on the right about 100m down. Some 30m **before** the tree, follow a path into the woods to your right; you soon see red waymarks to give you courage. After a long, winding traverse, climb to a further col (Peyris) and see another marker post. At this point, you may like to leave the path and follow yellow waymarks to the left for a few minutes to the Roc de Peyris, from where there are again superb views of the Gorges d'Héric. Return to the main path by the same route.

Head south again to reach a plateau on the ridge; follow the red waymarks carefully and make a steep descent to the left, passing an abandoned mine, which looks like the entrance to a cave. Eventually, start a steep drop down the southern slope through oak trees and across rocks. The path then bears southwest, between two ruined buildings, crosses a chestnut wood with a lot of very impressive dry-stone walling and enters **Mons**. Abandon the red waymarks, and go down the cement alley-way to the church.

Walk 12 – Les Gorges d'Héric

Distance:	14km
Time:	5h30
Total ascent:	880m
Grade:	B/C
Start point:	near Verdier
Map:	IGN 2543 ouest (St Gervais)

An exciting walk into the heart of the Caroux massif, requiring good hillcraft and a fair bit of stamina to deal with the change in height, but the views into the gorge and across to the south and west are ample reward. The sheer cliffs of the Gorges d'Héric rise 800m from the stream bed to the Caroux plateau, and the upward route, a combination of two paths known as the Sentier des Gardes and the Piste des Aiguilles, takes you from bottom to top, mostly through the welcome shade of evergreen oaks, across the Caroux plateau and down to the isolated stone-built hamlet of Héric, where there is a café. A short hop across the col to another ancient village, Bardou, brings you to a long, gently descending woodland path that returns you to Mons.

How to get there Travelling by car on the D908 from Lamalou les Bains, turn right at Mons/La Trivalle and take the D14 E32 to Le Verdier. Just beyond the hamlet, come to a car park (parking charge in season).

The route Go back past the snack bar and up the slope out of the car park. A few metres up, turn sharp right into the gorge road. Walk along the road into the gorge until you see a concrete footbridge (known as the 'Bridge of Sighs') across the stream. Go over the bridge and left to pick up an obvious path, waymarked with a blue triangle (Sentier des Gardes); the path soon starts to wind up the slope. Ignore a faintly waymarked right-hand path, and soon some red waymarks join the blue triangles. Keep on up the hillside to reach a junction with a blue-waymarked path, the Piste des Triangles; stay on the Sentier des Gardes and make your way ever upwards. Take a few moments to enjoy the fine views down into the gorge: west to the Roc de Peyris and the peak of **La Gleizo** (see Walk 11), and northwest up to the Fourcat d'Héric. Further up, the view opens to the south, right down to the Pyrenees.

As a long series of hairpin bends comes to an end at the **Col de Bartouyre**, go left on to a path heading north (red waymarks, blue cross). This is the Piste des Aiguilles. It meanders through the trees and is comfortingly well waymarked. Go up through the trees to a first ridge. Here, there are staggering views of the peaks around the gorge, including the impressive Roc de Bartouyre jutting out behind you. The path goes up and down and through a series of three gaps in the rocks; after the third one, drop down into a ravine to a junction with the Piste des Triangles coming up from the left.

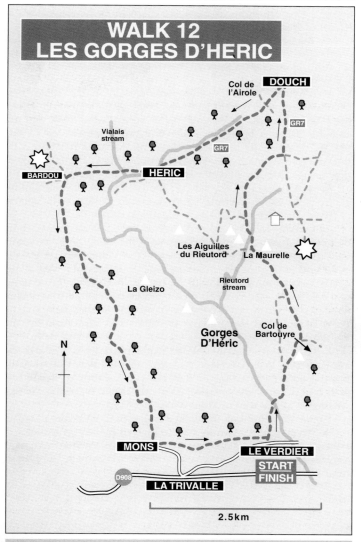

Emerging briefly from the trees, see the wall of the **Aiguilles du Rieutord** ahead and the peak of **La Maurelle** up to your right.

As the sound of the **Rieutord stream** gets closer, see a blue-waymarked path going off to the right (Piste Supérieur du Rieutord); follow it up through the woods to the stream at a point where it cascades over a ledge. Cross the stream and climb the slope to a junction with a yellow-waymarked path (Piste des Charbonniers). Head right and soon come up to a junction where the blue waymarks point you to the right. Leave them and go straight on up a broad track heading north-northeast onto the plateau. It gradually turns eastwards and reaches a junction with the GR7 (red/white markings). Go left onto the GR7 and follow it down, soon through a beech wood, towards the village of **Douch**.

Some 150m before the village, the GR7 turns left and climbs gently to the **Col de l'Airole** before descending towards the village of **Héric**. The path contains no navigational difficulties.

On arriving in Héric, take advantage of the café accommodation on offer in season, then head west out of the village, following the GR7 (red/white markings). Soon, cross the **Vialais stream** over a stone bridge. Go steadily up through chestnut trees and, after a few bends, reach a junction of paths at the col de Bardou. (From here, make a detour off the track: take the blue-marked path north for about 5 minutes to reach a viewpoint offering a large panorama of the Vialais valley, the village of Héric and the Aiguilles du Rieutord.)

From the junction at the col de Bardou follow the GR7 marks for a further 20m to a fork. Here, go left on to a red-waymarked path, passing above the village of **Bardou**. Head south, go through a breach in the rock and carry on gently downhill, following the red waymarks all the way to **Mons**.

Come down through the village and, some 20m before the road to La Trivalle, turn left into an alley which passes beneath some houses. The path goes east, soon through vines (white waymarks) to reach the hamlet of Verdier-Haut. Follow the gorge road north to return to the car park.

Walk 13 – Circuit of Cambon

Distance:	8.5km
Time:	2h10
Total ascent:	170m
Grade:	A
Start point:	Cambon
Map:	IGN 2443 est (La Salvetat)

The drive up from Olargues to Cambon via the Col de Fontfroide is a treat in itself; each hairpin bend gives a new view across the mountains, and you soon become aware that you are leaving the Mediterranean climate and vegetation behind to enter an area that is positively Alpine. The village of Cambon reinforces the impression. Gone are the terracotta tiles of the south; it is very much a mountain village, with steeply sloping slate roofs and black tiles hung down the side walls of many houses.

After a gentle climb out of Cambon, this is a fairly level walk that follows the southern ridge of the Espinouse plateau along the watershed between the Mediterranean and the Atlantic, giving wonderful views to the south before descending through woodland to the Agout stream and back to Cambon. On the way home, stop off and meander round the ancient village of Olargues, reputed not only for its beauty but also for its chestnuts!

How to get there Reach Olargues on the D908 Lamalou les Bains to St Pons road. Just west of Olargues, turn right off this road and head north for a spectacular ride up the D14 to the Col de Fontfroide. At the Col take the D53 down to Cambon.

The route From the church in Cambon, follow the D53 and the GR71 long-distance path (red/white waymarks) for about 1km in the direction of Salvergues. About 200m after the junction with the La Payssière road, leave the road near a recently built house and follow a forest road to the right, uphill. Ignore all joining paths and climb to reach a broad crossing path. Go left (southeast) and walk above a stream to a broad forest road, forming part of the **GR7** (red/white waymarks), at the edge of a beechwood. Turn right onto the road to reach the summit of the **Roc de l'Escayrou**, from which there are fine views of the Jaur valley, foothills of the Espinouse and the Mediterranean coastline.

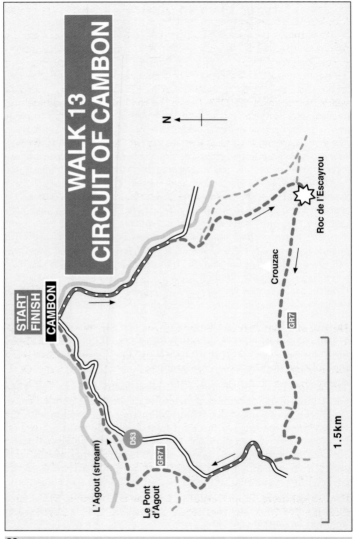

WALK 13
CIRCUIT OF CAMBON

START
FINISH
CAMBON

N

L'Agout (stream)

Le Pont
d'Agout

GR71

D53

GR7

Crouzac

Roc de l'Escayrou

1.5km

Follow the ridge westwards. This section forms part of the Mediterranean/Atlantic watershed.

Eventually, the forest road reaches the D53. Turn right onto the road and head north for about 1km; at a junction with the road to Lacout leave the D53 and pick up the **GR71** (red/white waymarks) below the minor road. Go through an enclosure and walk some 250m to the hamlet of **Le Pont d'Agout**. Go up the access road as it heads east to meet the D53. Leave the road almost immediately to join an obvious path on the left that drops through the woods. After about 100m, ignore the left-hand track that descends to a field and carry straight on, soon to follow the Agout stream into **Cambon**.

Walk 14 – Summit of Mont de l'Espinouse

Distance:	20.1km
Time:	6h30
Total ascent:	750m
Grade:	B/C
Start point:	Pont de Nougayrol, near Castanet le Haut
Map:	IGN 2543 ouest (St Gervais)

The summit of the Mont de l'Espinouse, though hidden by pine trees, is the highest point in the Hérault area (1124m), and the route, a combination of woodland, open plateau and exposed ridges, gives splendid views of the surrounding countryside, including the valley of the Vialais. The Saint-Eutrope ridge provides an early challenge – in fact, some knowledge of basic scrambling techniques is advisable in order to negotiate it safely. The Plo des Brus was once a Roman stronghold that guarded an important road joining the Rouergue area to the Mediterranean plain. A very basic refuge is available at Nostre Seigne. In order to avoid entering the national wildlife reserve the route has to follow the road for some 3km. However, the surrounding views are so lovely that you may not notice the tarmac, and there is certainly very little traffic.

How to get there From Hérépian, take the D13 north to St Gervais, then the D922 to Andabre. Here, follow the D22 E12 (towards

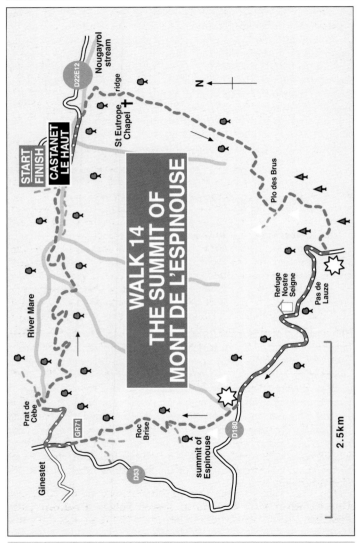

WALK 14
THE SUMMIT OF
MONT DE L'ESPINOUSE

START
FINISH
CASTANET
LE HAUT

D22E12

Nougayrol stream

St Eutrope Chapel
ridge

N

Plo des Brus

Refuge Nostre Seigne

Pas de Lauze

River Mare

Prat de Cèbe

GR71

Ginestet

D53

Roc Brise

summit of Espinouse

D180

2.5km

Castanet le Haut) alongside the River Mare. About 1km from Castanet, find a bridge (the Pont de Nougayrol). Park here.

The route Follow a waymarked track eastwards (red/yellow) for about 250m. Look carefully for a path which goes off to the right through chestnut trees, heading southeast. On reaching a ruin, find the ancient track; cross a stream (Devois de Fayet) and climb through a series of bends to a broad ridge. Climb up a rocky plinth to reach the **Chapel of Saint-Eutrope** (there is an annual pilgrimage to this chapel at the end of April).

Heading south, go through a gap and alongside a vertical rock-face. Take great care at this point, as the ancient track has almost disappeared. Climb the eastern slope above a stream (Ruisseau de Salibens), about 30m from the crest of the ridge. Pass through a series of gaps along a steep, overgrown slope and arrive at a col (note the reddish, broken rock). Climb to the right, up the western slope and along a rocky path bordered with heather and broom, occasionally glimpsing sections of the ancient track.

Amongst some beech trees you arrive at an obvious col; on the other side, go southwest through the trees alongside a rock-face; upstream, rejoin the crest of the ridge and go on to a grassy plateau. Head southwest to attain the highest point of the Saint-Eutrope ridge. Follow the ridge-path west, then drop to the left to meet a wide track by some ruins. Go along this track, climbing south to a fork at the **Plo des Brus** (this is an old Roman outpost which guarded the trade route between the Rouergue region and the Mediterranean plain).

Go left along a flat dirt road; in the forest descend gently to the road (D180) at a **viewpoint** which looks down on to the valley of the Vialais. Turn right on to the road and follow it for 3.5km, passing the Pas de Lauze and a **refuge** (Nostre Seigne). The road then crosses the wooded plateau of the Plo du Flamboyau. At a long left-hand bend, about 45 minutes from the Pas de Lauze, leave the road to climb to the right up a forest track, which soon turns northeast to pass 50m to the east of the **summit of Espinouse**, now hidden amongst pine trees.

Descend rapidly north to a fork (**Roc Brise**); continue right and cross the River Mare close to its source. Follow a balcony path north, then west to a junction with the GR71 long-distance path (red/white waymarks). Follow this, descending right to a grassy plateau and a road (D53). Go some 300m down the road to a junction at a col.

To the right, follow the little road leading to a farm (**Prat de Cèbe** – water available) and continue north, crossing a stream; along a dirt road go right to re-cross the stream and pass below the farm. Follow the stream downhill through a series of bends to reach an area of flat ground. About 500m further on, leave the track and head left along the old track, which crosses the Mare before reaching the first houses of **Castanet le Haut**. Go down a narrow street below the church to reach a wide avenue. This leads to the D22 E12 and on to the bridge.

Walk 15 – Circuit of Montahut

Distance:	12.8km
Time:	4h30
Total ascent:	820m
Grade:	B
Start point:	Les Castagnes
Map:	IGN 2543 ouest (St Gervais)

As you drive along the D908 between Mons/La Trivalle and Olargues, you can see the great rocky dome of Montahut (1053m) prominent on the Espinouse massif, with its neighbour, the Roc d'Ourliades, protruding some 300m to the west. The walk takes you up from the valley along the Cabrignous ridge to a col below the summit of Montahut, before following the ravine of the Chavardès stream back to Les Castagne. It offers a mix of woodland and open ridge walking with views down to Olargues and the Jaur Valley.

How to get there Take the D908 from Bedarieux, and between Mons/LaTrivalle and Olargues turn right onto the D14 E18 to arrive at the hamlet of Les Castagnes. Park near the Mairie.

The route With your back to the Mairie bear left (northwest) along a narrow road to reach a small concreted square above the village.

The Roc de Caroux from La Gleizo (Walk 13)

The medieval village of Olargues, with Mont Caroux behind (Walk 15)

The Espinouse and Caroux from Mont Sialassous (Walk 16)

One of the windmills at Faugères, restored to working order (Walk 25)

Mont Liausson, dominating the Cirque de Mourèze (Walks 26 & 27)

From Mont Liausson, looking across the Lac du Salagou (Walk 27)

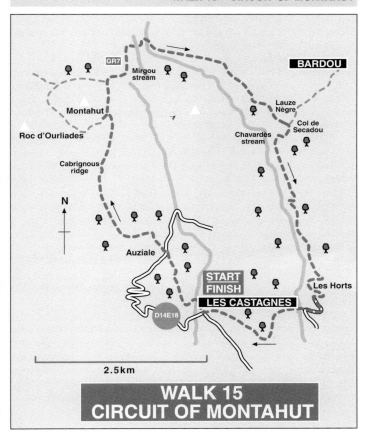

**WALK 15
CIRCUIT OF MONTAHUT**

Head north up a stone path beside a concrete drive and cross the stream by a footbridge. Start to climb, and at the second bend (blue-painted rock) do **not** go straight on; instead, climb to the right along an old sheep-drovers' track which takes you across the D14 E31 and, twice, over a concrete lane. Soon arrive for a third time at the concrete lane, and turn left to arrive at the hamlet of **Auziale**. Walk through the hamlet for about 80m then take a narrow alley to the left, which leads to a junction above the houses. Continue north along a good track and to the left of a reservoir (a grassy hump next to a small building).

On reaching a ridge go northwest; near a pointed rock, leave the wide track and head left to pick up an ancient track (red waymark). Follow this for 50m or so to a junction of paths; follow the red marks to the southwest and climb through heather and broom along a path lined with cairns. Continue along the ridge, beside a chestnut plantation, and reach a small col.

Follow a long wall north along the **Cabrignous ridge**; leave the wall just beyond a small ruined building to follow a sheepdrovers' path along the eastern slope. Soon this becomes a wide grassy track which you follow to a junction with the GR7 long-distance path (red/white waymarks). Go right onto the GR7 and watch for a left turn after about 80m, where the GR7 turns on to a narrow path which traverses northwest. Above a ruined sheep-fold, cross a stream and follow it down through the rocks. Go over the next stream (**Mirgou**) and, a few metres higher, continue along the GR7 as it traverses to the east above the stream of Chavardes. At the col (**Lauze Nègre**), marked by a large rock outcrop, wind your way down the ridges of the southern slope (southeast) to reach the **Col de Secadou** amongst chestnut trees.

At this point you leave the GR7; go right to pass some recently restored stone dwellings and wind your way down a concrete road for about 25 minutes to reach the hamlet of **Les Horts**. Walk through the village and continue along the D14 E19. At a bend, leave the road and follow a track through vines towards a stone hut. Cross the stream by a bridge behind the hut and climb south at first, then turn right on to a concrete track to arrive soon at **Les Castagnes**.

Walk 16 – Les Sagnes

Distance:	7.4km
Time:	2 hours
Total ascent:	220m
Grade:	A
Start point:	Olargues
Map:	IGN 2543 ouest (St Gervais)

A varied, airy and easy walk offering fine views over the village of Olargues as well as a chance to explore the village's ancient cobbled streets, stone staircases, 11th-century bell-tower and 13th-century bridge, Pont du Diable. To the north and east, views up to the Roc d'Ourliades and Caroux are breathtaking. Les Sagnes is a tiny hamlet at the halfway point of the walk, looking down over Olargues.

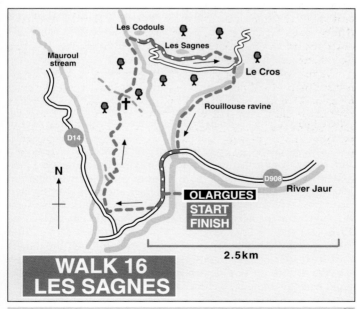

How to get there Take the D908 from Lamalou to Olargues; go into the centre of the village and park opposite the Mairie in Place Alexandre-Laissac.

The route Go to the corner of the square at the left-hand end of the Mairie and go left through the 13th-century Porte Neuve. Continue up the Rue Neuve into the village, then descend the Rue de la Place (see Escalier de la Commanderie to the right). Go on down the Rue de la Comporte and right into the Rue du long de la Muraille. Then take the Rue des Moulins and cross the River Jaur via the 13th-century Pont du Diable. Turn left along the D908 for about 200m, then turn right just before a petrol station (Faubourg du Gué) and walk up a concrete lane. Beyond the dwellings, reach a junction and go right. Soon the concrete ends and you are on an unmade road.

Ignore a vineyard track to the right and, at a fork, climb to the right on an unmade road. As you climb, see the pointed Roc d'Ourliades ahead. Continue to climb, following the line of the stream (**Mauroul**). Ignore another vineyard track to the left, and then ignore a second track which leads to the Mas du Gua, way off to the left at the far end of the valley. At the next fork, ignore the blue waymarks and follow a winding path upwards.

At the next junction fork left by some vines. The Roc d'Ourliades is high above you, straight ahead, the vast bulk of Caroux is off to your right and there is a long view down the valley, ending with the pointed peak of Tantajo, which sits above Bédarieux. Arrive at a junction at the Col de St Martin des Oeufs, where there is a small **chapel** with an altar and a few frescoes, but no eggs!

From the chapel go up to the right past a stand of fir trees. At a fork some 200m further on, ignore the waymarked downward path and go up through chestnut trees. Pass under an electricity line and soon arrive at a narrow lane. Go right then, shortly, ignore the left-hand road which leads to the hamlet of **Les Codouls**. Go straight on, then left at the next junction. Down to the right you can see the River Jaur and the Pont du Diable which you crossed earlier. After 300m, reach the hamlet of **Les Sagnes**. Walk through the hamlet and, soon after, ignore a right-hand descending road and go uphill for 30m to pick up an old path going off to the right along a left-hand wall (terracing for a cherry orchard).

The 13th-century Pont du Diable spans the River Jaur at Olargues

Drop down to the hamlet of **Le Cros**; turn right, then descend left and walk southwards through the hamlet. Carry on in the same direction on a cement track through vines, with the church tower of Olargues ahead. As you descend, the Roc d'Ourliades appears again to your right. At a junction with a concrete road bear right into a ravine (**Rouillouse**). Come down to the D908. Turn right and walk some 500m back to the Pont du Diable, over the bridge and back to the village via the Rue du Pont Vieux and the Rue Neuve.

Walk 17 – Circuit of Coustorgues

Distance:	17.5 km
Time:	5h45
Total ascent:	830m
Grade:	B/C
Start point:	Le Cros de St Vincent d'Olargues
Map:	IGN 2443 est (La Salvetat) and 2444 est (St Pons)

A strenuous walk with plenty of uphill work on the outward stretch, but you are rewarded with excellent views to the south across the Jaur valley and across the Espinouse massif. The hamlet of Coustorgues is situated in a great bowl of woodland between Mont Sialassous and the Espinouse massif. A quiet spot for most of the year, the area is invaded in early October by hordes of mushroom-pickers from all over the Languedoc. There is a lot of woodland walking, but once up on Sialassous the terrain is open and airy.

How to get there Approach the hamlet of Le Cros de St Vincent d'Olargues via the D908 or the D14 and then the D14 E14; from Le Cros take the D14 E15 towards Violgues and Pestous. After about 100m, park just before the bridge over the Coustorgues stream.

The route Walk back along the D14 E15 for about 100m towards **Le Cros**; pick up an old track to the left which brings you back to the north on the left bank of the stream (**Coustorgues**). Cross the stream just below a ruined bridge, then climb upstream to a fork. Bear right and cross another stream (**Cabriol**) and head north up the Coustorgues stream for about 250m, crossing it once. The path is blocked at this point and you should turn left into a meadow to rejoin the stream at the corner of a wired enclosure. Cross over again and go north to reach an unmade road leading to a large field. Follow this wide track along the edge of a chestnut plantation and round two bends to reach a fork; go straight on (northwest) to arrive at **Coustorgues**.

Cross the stream and find a cemented alley-way which takes you up above the houses; cross a stream and climb immediately to the right. Then, leave Coustorgues along a left-hand track, soon to reach a fork amongst the chestnut trees. Take a good track to the right and then a path which crosses a stream (**Bosc Nègre**).

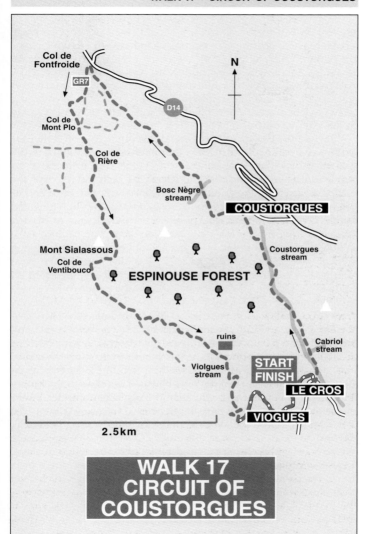

N

Col de
Fontfroide

GR7

D14

Col de
Mont Plo

Col de
Rière

Bosc Nègre
stream

COUSTORGUES

Mont Sialassous

Col de
Ventibouco

Coustorgues
stream

ESPINOUSE FOREST

ruins

Cabriol
stream

Violgues
stream

START
FINISH

LE CROS

VIOGUES

2.5km

WALK 17
CIRCUIT OF
COUSTORGUES

Some often faint green waymarking guides you all the way to the Col de Fontfroide, which you should reach in about an hour. Looking over a stream (Campeyria), abandon the path which goes up its right bank and go left up a winding track which climbs north to a ridge. Ignoring a second northward path arrive at a crest and a col (green waymark on a white quartz block). Bear right onto an old track and climb gradually northeast to a beechwood. On emerging from the wood, cross a pine plantation and, 100m further on, arrive at the **Col de Fontfroide** near two information boards.

Beyond the boards follow a broad track that goes off to the left (red/white waymarks denoting the long-distance footpath GR7) and climbs southwest to another col (**Mont Plo**); from there, go right (south). At the next col (**de Rière**) the path forks. Leave the GR7 and take the track southwest along the ridge, passing a barrier after about 80m. The track soon starts to descend through pine and beech. Look out for a broad, grassy track which rises to the left (through a gap in the trees you will see some thin radio masts). Follow this straight uphill and, just before you reach the top, look right to see the corner of a fence. Follow this fence to the right (southwest) to come alongside the masts at the top of the **Mont du Sialassous**. Continue along the fence-line – the path is very narrow and overgrown here – until you reach the corner of the enclosure. Dive off to the rocks on your left to enjoy fabulous views across to the Espinouse and Caroux, then come back to the fence-corner and follow the line of the fence southwest and down to a wide track.

Follow this track down to its low point. Go up the bank (cairn) and, at the edge of a clump of beeches, join the old route which descends south to the **Col de Ventibouco**. Walk though the broom over the col. Do not follow the ridge – drop down into the valley (southeast) and, amongst trees, reach a fork. Downwards and to the left, take an obvious path which winds down to a stream (**Ruisseau de Violgues**), close to some sheepfolds. Continue on a good track which soon leaves the stream and drops onto the southern slope. Descend through chestnut trees and wind your way down on a broad track to the hamlet of **Violgues**. Go east through the hamlet and walk some 1.6km along the D14 E15 to return to your car.

Walk 18 – Circuit of Cassagnoles

Distance:	6km
Time:	1h45
Total ascent:	150m
Grade:	A
Start point:	Cassagnoles
Map:	IGN 2444 est (St Pons)

A short, gentle ramble out from the hamlet of Cassagnoles, with lovely views across the Somail mountain and a mix of open land, vines and woodland to walk through.

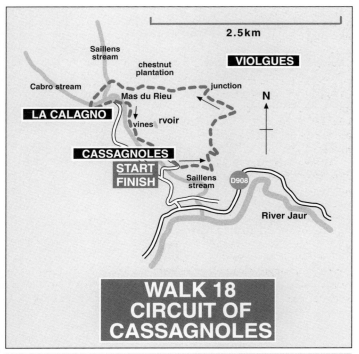

**WALK 18
CIRCUIT OF
CASSAGNOLES**

How to get there Access to the hamlet of Cassagnoles by car is from the D908 Lamalou les Bains to St Pons road; about 1km northeast of St Etienne d'Albagnan take a narrow road to Cassagnoles. Park just outside the village.

The route Go through **Cassagnoles** and, at the other side, go left along an unmade road. Cross a low point in the valley and continue southeast along a path which looks over a stream (**Ruisseau de Saillens**). Come to another path which climbs across the slope. Go up to the left and follow northwest a broad track hollowed out of the rock. Two sharp bends lead to a long curve, then cross the valley of Gaillergues to reach a ridge.

Head northwest to a junction to the south of Violgues. Climb rapidly to the left and after 250m reach another junction at a col. Go up to the right for about 50m, then left (west). Go through some vines above a little farmhouse and follow a good path into a chestnut plantation to cross a stream (Saillens) – a good picnic spot.

Go upstream to reach **La Calagno** just beyond the Cabro stream. Descend left at the corner of the first building to a chestnut plantation. Ignore a left-hand path; the broad, winding track comes out at a minor road. To the left, cross a bridge and walk to the **Mas du Rieu** (farm).

Follow the Ruisseau de Saillens along a broad track south to reach a fork. Descend right on an unmade road which goes through some vines, then climbs to a small promontory and a fork. An excellent balcony path (southeast, 350m) brings you back to **Cassagnoles**.

Walk 19 – Le Saut de Vézoles

Distance:	6km
Time:	1h30
Total ascent:	40m
Grade:	A
Start point:	Col de Cabarétou
Map:	IGN 2444 est (St Pons)

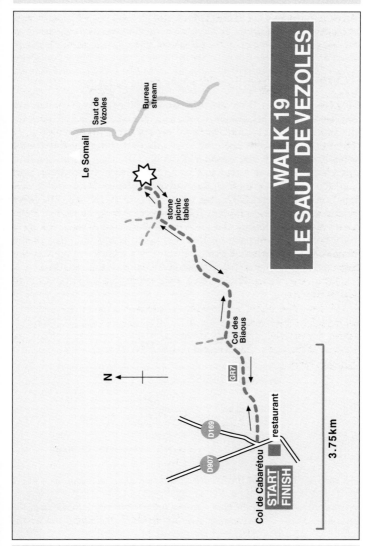

**WALK 19
LE SAUT DE VEZOLES**

An easy walk along a flat, broad forest road on the Somail plateau to look at the spectacular Saut de Vezoles, where the Bureau stream flows out of the Lac de Vézoles and cascades some 200m over gigantic granite boulders down the almost sheer face of Le Somail before joining the River Jaur 700m below. There are some striking views down the Jaur valley towards Caroux on the way. This is not a circuit – simply retrace your steps.

How to get there Take the D907 from St Pons or La Salvetat. On reaching the Col de Cabarétou, at a junction with the D169, park by the side of the road (there is a good restaurant 100m downhill).

The route Just below the junction, walk east along the **Cabarétou** forest track (red/white waymarks denote GR7 long-distance path). After 300m pass a forest lodge; ignore a right-hand track and continue east to a fork at the **Col des Biaous**. Bear right, still heading east on the GR7, and soon, on your right, see two **stone picnic tables**. Another 100m further on is a fork. Here, leave the forest track and follow the GR7 (red/white waymarks), taking a right-hand path into the heather. Go north along the edge of the plateau to a viewpoint. From here, there is a wonderful view of the **Saut de Vézoles**, Jaur valley and, on a clear day, the coastline.

From the viewpoint, retrace your steps back to the **Col de Cabarétou**.

Walk 20 – Le Priou

Distance:	13km
Time:	3 hours
Total ascent:	220m
Grade:	A
Start point:	Le Priou
Map:	IGN 2544 ouest (St Chinian)

An easy walk out from the hamlet of Le Priou along a broad, open forest road that contours round the summit of Montahuc. Yet it is hugely rewarding for the views it gives – south to the plain, the Pyrenees and the sea, north to the Caroux massif, west to the Montagne Noire, and for the

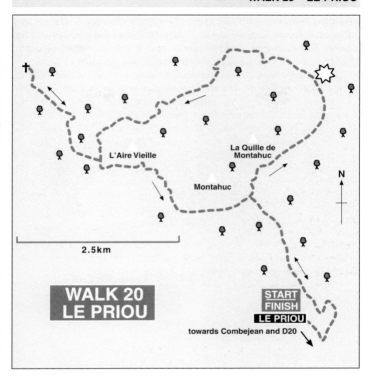

different types of landscape through which you travel – woodland, dry plateau and pasture. Waymarking is yellow throughout.

How to get there From Cessenon-sur-Orb take the D20 towards Saint-Chinian. A few kilometres from Saint-Chinian, turn right into Combejean. In the village turn left, and after some 200m turn right by a statue of the Sacred Heart and head for the hamlet of Le Priou. Park in the hamlet near the Domaine de Pradels winery.

The route Opposite the winery a broad track (waymarking is yellow throughout) climbs behind a stone barn and winds up the hillside. (If you are feeling very lazy you can take the car up and just walk the horizontal bit.) In about 40 minutes the track arrives at a junction on a small plateau. Go right and follow the track round the eastern flank of the hill. After terrific views down to the sea and to the Pyrenees, Caroux suddenly appears to the northeast.

About half-way round the circuit, on the north side of the hill, arrive at a junction with a narrow tarmac road. (At this point you can make a detour: if you turn right, the road leads you to the **Chapelle de la Dourque**, where there is a picnic area. Then retrace your steps to the junction – 4km total). Go straight on along the tarmac road and soon come to an area of grassland on a plateau. At a junction near a large cylindrical water tank, turn left onto a narrow concrete road and climb gradually to a point where you can see extensive views to both north and south. The route now descends gently to the right and contours round the south side of the hill to reach to junction with the track which brought you up from **Le Priou**. Retrace your steps to the hamlet.

Walk 21 – Circuit of Villemagne

Distance:	8km
Time:	2h45
Total ascent:	260m
Grade:	A
Map:	IGN 2543 est (Bédarieux)

The ancient village of Villemagne has played an important role in the history of the area and contains some interesting architecture, including Charlemagne's Mint. This varied walk, with no strenuous climbing, takes you up onto the Causse, a limestone plateau between Villemagne and Bédarieux, and offers good views over Villemagne and the plateau itself. You will see plenty of cherry orchards along the way, one of which covers a whole hillside – a wonder to behold in spring when the blossom comes out.

How to get there Reach Villemagne by the D922 from Hérépian. To the north side of the village is a wide avenue lined with plane trees. Park here.

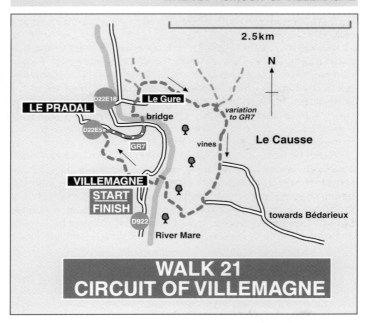

**WALK 21
CIRCUIT OF VILLEMAGNE**

The route Walk back along the D922 in the direction of Hérépian. At a left-hand bend, go right up a tarmac track. Climb gently, pass the cemetery entrance and keep going north. At a fork, go left up a steep slope, and 200m further on reach the St Martin Cross (the chapel here was destroyed in the 16th century). Carry on along the cement track to a fork; go right along a balcony path (north-northeast) and reach a road (D22 E5). Here is a junction with the GR7 long-distance path, marked in red/white. Follow the road and GR7 down and right to the D922. Cross over, go 30m left, find a gap in the parapet and cross the River Mare by the **Pont du Diable**.

Go left along a dirt track then, by a hut, bear right along a path which goes between two walls (north). After a short walk through undergrowth, bear left, cross the road (D22 E18) and wind your way up to the hamlet of **La Gure**. Leave the hamlet to the right, and carry on north, then east close to a large building. Go up along a track which is cement at first, then becomes a dirt road, to reach a fork.

Leave the main GR7 (which heads off north towards Boussagues) and follow instead the alternative route (signed *variante*) which heads east and leads to Bédarieux. This is marked in red and white and forms a long, gently climbing traverse of the north slopes of the Issartels hills; there are good views of the Mare valley, Caroux and Villemagne. You will come eventually to a wide col and a junction of paths. Here there are more splendid views, this time of the foothills, Tantajo and the Causse.

Go right along a wide track (pink waymarks, irregular). After a low wall descend immediately left, cross a vineyard and head south, slowly losing height. Ignore tracks to right and left (entrances to properties), and enter a second vineyard. Go round it to the left and soon reach a fork, marked with a cross. Continue straight on, south, alongside fenced land and then along the edge of a cherry orchard. Ignore a left-hand track which goes off into a stand of trees, and at the south end of the orchard reach a tarmac track on the left.

Go south (right) and at a small col ignore a left-hand cement track. The winding path goes through a valley and turns north, soon offering a delightful balcony view of **Villemagne**. Go down to the footbridge and cross the river to reach the village.

Walk 22 – Pic de la Coquillade

Distance:	12km
Time:	4 hours
Total ascent:	450m
Grade:	B
Start point:	Cabrerolles
Map:	IGN 2544 est (Murviel)

To the south of the Caroux massif is a line of wooded foothills going from west to east, sheltering the vineyards on the Mediterranean plain. These hills are known as the Avant-Monts, and one of the most interesting, as

La Coquillade

La Borie Nouvelle

Col de la Balque

N

CABREROLLES
START
FINISH

D136E4   D154

2.5km

WALK 22
PIC DE LA COQUILLADE

well as one of the highest, is the Pic de la Coquillade. Topped by a number of communications masts, the peak gives a full 360° view – taking in the coastal plain and the sea to the south and the mountains of Caroux and Espinouse to the north. The starting point is the pretty hamlet of Cabrerolles with its ancient castle and chapel, nestling in a wooded ravine and surrounded by vineyards, and the walk winds gently up through the shade of evergreen oaks to the open summit.

How to get there From the main D909 Béziers to Bédarieux road, take either the D136 E4 or the D154 westwards to the village of Cabrerolles. Park near the Mairie.

The route Facing the cemetery, walk up the right-hand road which takes you up through the village. At the top, follow a path (waymarking is yellow) which leads to the ruins of the old chateau and then the **chapel**. The castle ruins date from the 10th century, the chapel from the 11th, and were built alongside an ancient trade route between the Aveyron and the plain of Béziers. Once destroyed, then rebuilt and abandoned, the chapel is in the process of being restored by a committee of local people.

Beyond the chapel find a path with blue waymarks which climbs through the woods. When this path meets a forestry track, fork right, then left on a tarmac road. When you reach the hamlet of **La Borie Nouvelle**, after the first house take a left-hand track which descends a little before turning right and climbing to rejoin the forestry track. Go right, and head for the summit of **La Coquillade**. Take time to enjoy the views from here: to the north you can see Caroux, Espinouse and Lamalou; and to the south are visible the Pyrenees and the whole plain of Béziers with the sea beyond.

Just below the summit, look for and follow a steeply descending left-hand path; follow the blue waymarking carefully as it goes up and down through the trees. Soon reach a junction of paths; follow the blue marks to the left and descend to the stony plateau of the **Col de la Balque**, with a small rock face ahead. Go straight on and climb up behind the rock wall, then follow the narrow but well-marked path as it winds up and down through tall trees before emerging into a mix of evergreen oak and box.

Keeping a careful eye on the blue waymarks, start to descend the hillside, enjoying a view of some of the Faugères vineyards, where the vines are planted on terraces which follow the contours of the slopes. The AOC (Appellation d'Origine Contrôlée) wines of Faugères are becoming justifiably well-known throughout Europe and America. Produced in the villages of Faugères, Autignac, Cabrerolles, Caussiniojouls, Laurens, Roquessels and Fos, they are well worth a *dégustation* – after the walk! Eventually, walk alongside a wall down an old drovers' track, bear left and arrive back at the cemetery at **Cabrerolles**.

Walk 23 – La Maurelle

Distance:	17km
Time:	5 hours
Total ascent:	350m
Grade:	B
Start point:	Caveau des Schistes, near Laurens
Maps:	IGN 2544 est (Murviel) and 2543 est (Bédarieux)

This circuit of a hill known as La Maurelle can be a walk or, if you have brought your mountain bike, a strenuous ride. As well as passing close to the villages of Laurens and Caussiniojouls, you also get a flavour of the Faugères vineyards and the oak woods that cover the foothills. From the highest point there are splendid views of the coastal plain, the Pyrenees, and the mountains Caroux and Espinouse.

The church in the village of Caussiniojouls

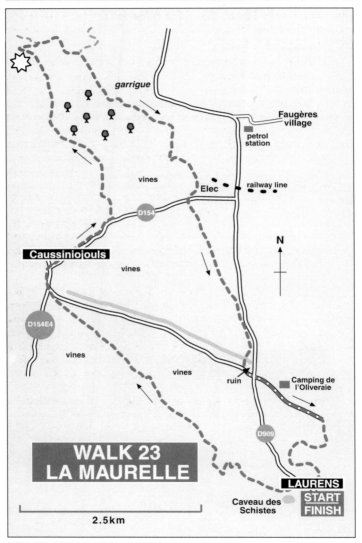

garrigue

Faugères
village

petrol
station

vines

Elec

railway line

D154

N

Caussiniojouls

vines

vines

D154E4

vines

vines

ruin

Camping de
l'Oliveraie

D909

WALK 23
LA MAURELLE

LAURENS
START
FINISH

Caveau des
Schistes

2.5km

How to get there On the main D909 Béziers to Bédarieux road, just opposite the village of Laurens, find the Caveau des Schistes, a sales point for wine, and park there.

The route From the Caveau des Schistes follow the tarmac lane to the right of the building, over a ford. Follow the yellow waymarks onto a dirt road; keep going for about 2km through vines and woodland until the track joins a tarmac surface. This brings you down to a road, with the village of **Caussiniojouls** ahead, its church in the foreground. Just before the church, turn right onto the road signed 'Faugères' (D154) and walk for about 1.5km. At an oak tree, the yellow markings indicate a left turn up a narrow tarmac lane.

Shortly, bear right onto a wide dirt track; on reaching the woods, go right then left, and follow the track as it winds up to the top of the hill. Enjoy wide views when you get there. Bear right by a large metal container. As you start to descend, find a left fork which takes you towards the oak woods, then turn left along a track bordered by walls (this is part of an old drove road). Come out of the woods and cross a section of *garrigue*, the local term for scrubland (you will see the main D909 to your left, with the Faugères tourist bureau and wine sales point).

Go right along a dirt track, then alongside a railway line. At the road (D154) go left, pass an EDF (electricity) **substation** and turn right onto a tarmac road. At an old almond tree bear left and follow the waymarks along a vineyard track. At the far end go into the wood and down to a stream. Cross it, go past a well, cut across a tarmac track and, by a 'stop' sign, climb up towards the trees. Here you'll find a ruin (old coaching inn), now being restored. Go over a ford and fork right, then left.

Cross the D909 and walk up the road opposite, soon passing the Camping de l'Oliveraie. Some 500m further on, fork right onto a dirt track which climbs up a short hill before dropping down to the road opposite the **Caveau des Schistes**.

Walk 24 – Les Trois Tours

(The Three Towers)

Distance:	13.3 km
Time:	4 hours
Total ascent:	300m
Grade:	A/B
Start point:	Faugères
Map:	IGN 2543 est (Bedarieux)

A delightful walk through vineyards, woods and onto the hilltops surrounding Faugères. The 'three towers', once windmills (currently being restored – one in operation), on the summit above Faugères are the focal point of the walk; from this peak, a huge view opens out across the plain to the coast. On returning to the village, you can spend a very pleasant half-hour exploring the narrow streets of the old centre before slipping up the road to the Bel Air for a beer or a meal. (The petrol station opposite has the best stock of local wines in the area – ask to see the back room!)

How to get there From the main Béziers to Bédarieux road, join Faugères by the D13. Park in a little square opposite the old village.

The route Walk down the main road (D13) in the direction of Pézenas; just after a little *tabac*, go left between the last two houses along a tarmac lane. Where the lane becomes cemented, ignore the left fork and continue uphill. At a junction by a new plantation of olive trees, continue left on a tarmac road, ignoring a right turn some 50m further on. The track winds upwards to reach another fork on a wide brow. Go straight on, between vineyards, with a stone wall on your left, and follow the road through an oak wood and across a very attractive valley planted with vines.

   The road then drops briefly into the combe (**Combe Gastouse**), then climbs up to a junction. Go left (north) and soon pass a stone barn. Carry on and pass two more barns to reach a junction. Here, descend left (north) and follow the tarmac track for 150m to a fork. Turn left onto a dirt track which descends then climbs past a stone house (**Mas Rouch**). Ignore a narrow left-hand path and continue to climb steadily. As the path levels out, see a second left-hand path (look for a blue waymark on a tree 5m down the path) and follow it

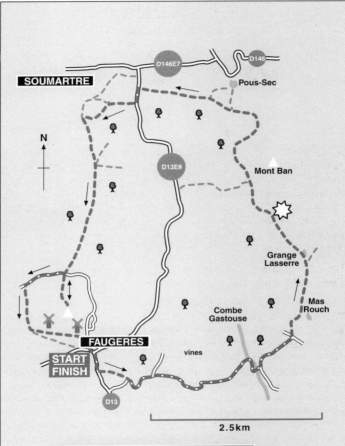

SOUMARTRE

D146E7

D146

Pous-Sec

N

D13E8

Mont Ban

Grange
Lasserre

Mas
Rouch

Combe
Gastouse

FAUGERES

vines

START
FINISH

D13

2.5km

WALK 24
LES TROIS TOURS
(THREE TOWERS)

Two of the 'three towers': the windmills of Faugères were restored in the 1990s and are producing flour once again

past the ruins of a stone barn (**Grange Lasserre**). Carry on through the trees to the head of the valley. At a junction of paths, go right along a good path which climbs up through the wood to a small col. From here, enjoy the great view of the Pic de Tantajo, Caroux, the Faugères windmills and the other foothills.

A short descent brings you to a fork at a point where, in times past, charcoal burners worked. Keep straight on along a magnificent contour path which takes you round below the summit of **Mont Ban**. Descend soon to a white gate, then reach a clearing. Go northwest on a wide track, ignoring a track right which leads to **Pous-Sec** pottery (but do visit there another day – it's superb). Eventually, you come to a road (D13 E8). Turn left and follow it for 250m, then go right along a wide dirt track. At a fork, bear left, uphill, and after short walk through vines reach a junction with a lane bordered by hedges.

Go left and follow the lane to a plateau. Ahead you will see the **windmills** of Faugères on the hill-top. From a junction, a wide track takes you up to them and a wonderful view on all sides.

Come back down the hill to the junction, turn left on to the road and head west for some 500m. Turn left onto a wide stone track with a wooden barrier. On your left are two excellent examples of *capitelles* – old dry-stone shelters used by farmers centuries ago; a local history group has been rebuilding them in this area. Descend to a fork, bear left, and drop down to cross the valley bottom. About 200m further on, look carefully for the start – on your left – of an old path (red waymarks) which takes you between stone walls, past another *capitelle*, and soon on to **Faugères**. Take time to amble around the old village before rejoining your car.

Many of the old capitelles – dry-stone shelters once used by farmers – are being restored around Faugères

Walk 25 – Tour of Mont Liausson

Distance:	8km
Time:	2h30
Total ascent:	270m
Grade:	A
Start point:	Mourèze
Map:	IGN 2643 ouest (Lodève)

Mont Liausson is an impressive 500m-high limestone ridge standing between the Cirque de Mourèze (an extraordinary chaos of dolomitic rock eroded into fascinating shapes – the Sphinx, the Camel, the Sleeping Lion) and the Lac du Salagou, an enormous man-made lake created in the late 1960s. This walk, a mix of open and woodland trails, does not involve any strenuous climbing as you are not going to the top of the mountain, merely contouring round it. Yet it affords wonderful views of the Mediterranean coastline, the lake and surrounding countryside and takes you through the heart of the Cirque itself. The village of Mourèze is well worth a visit for its picturesque centre and for the Parc des Courtinals, a reconstruction of an ancient Gallic settlement.

How to get there The village of Mourèze is signposted off the main D908 Bédarieux to Clermont l'Hérault road. Park as close to the village centre as you can.

The route Walk from the main road up through the old part of the village, following signs for the Cirque. Just after the last house, ignore the left-hand path (Col de Portes) and carry on towards the Cirque. Follow the line of a wire fence down to a low point. Looking northeast, you should spot some blue waymarks. Follow this path through a narrow ravine, heading towards an outcrop of rock with a large bulbous head – this is known as **the Sphinx**. About 50m before the Sphinx, the waymarks guide you sharply to the left. Climb gradually, keeping the Sphinx on your right. Soon the path flattens after a further climb and descent to reach the foot of Mont Liausson. Shortly, pass between two large rocks and reach some pine trees and scrub. Look back 180 degrees to see the pointed head of the Pic de Vissou which towers above the vineyards of Cabrières (the *caveau* is well worth a visit on the way home).

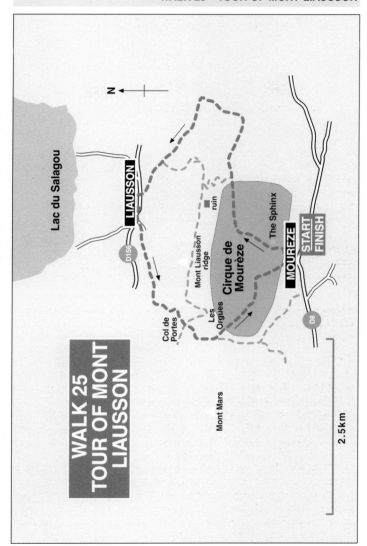

WALK 25
TOUR OF MONT
LIAUSSON

Lac du Salagou

LIAUSSON

D156

Col de Portes

Les Orgues

Mont Liausson ridge

ruin

Cirque de Mourèze

The Sphinx

MOURÈZE

START FINISH

D8

Mont Mars

2.5km

N

Part of the Cirque de Mourèze, this unusual rock formation is known as the Sphinx

Turning eastwards, the path now points you towards the eastern end of the mountain. A gentle climb of some 300m brings you to a junction of paths. Go right, and soon a fine view of Mourèze and the Cirque opens up. Continuing further up, you begin to see the coastline and the rounded hill of Sète. At the next junction look for signs pointing right to Anse and Gorges des Combasses (Walk 26 breaks away here). Follow this path downwards for a time and then up to a col, from which splendid views open up to the east. In the distance is the pointed summit of the Pic St Loup, north of Montpellier.

The path winds down now in a general northeasterly direction. In spring, the air is heady here with the scent of thyme, rosemary and gorse – take it all in, then climb to another col. Another wonderful view greets you, this time of the Lac du Salagou. If the north wind is blowing, you'll have been protected from it so far, but it will catch you here! Follow the path right – it then starts to wind down in the direction of the lake. Waymarks change to red as you reach a junction (small cairn) with a right-hand path; go left, with the lake on your right, through some tall pines. Soon the path broadens out and the spire of the church at **Liausson** is seen ahead. Go down into the village and, at the road, turn left and head out of the village. On a telegraph pole, spot a yellow waymark which guides you left up a narrow road. This shortly becomes a track. Follow the yellow waymarks.

At a fork, go left and climb gently to another fork by a stone wall. Go right, between wall and vineyard, then the path curves right and uphill. Here begins a longish slog up to the **Col de Portes**, with the huge limestone cliff of the Mont Liausson on your left. Just when you've had enough, you reach the col, where there is a junction of four paths (Walk 27 joins here). Go straight on downhill (blue waymarks) towards Mourèze. After a steep descent the path curves left and in front of you are the huge, fluted limestone outcrops which form the western edge of Mont Liausson. These are known as **Les Orgues** – presumably someone thought they looked like organ-pipes. The wide track descends gently now and the Pic de Vissou soon comes into view ahead. At this point **watch carefully** for a small sign which indicates a narrow left-hand path (blue waymarks). Take this path, which leads you up to a col near Les Orgues. Go past a large rock with a hole in it and you reach the western edge of the **Cirque de Mourèze**. Keep your eyes open for blue marks, cross another col and the village of Mourèze comes into view.

The path is now a balcony walk beneath the cliffs, and a broad view of the Cirque is gained. Then, gradually move away from the mountain and down into the Cirque. Twisting and turning through the rocks, the path comes down to a small canyon lined with pine, rosemary, gorse and heather. Pass under an overhanging cliff and through a tunnel of trees, and you emerge at the entrance to the Cirque. A short walk back through the village will return you to **Mourèze** and your car.

Walk 26 – The Mont Liausson Ridge

Distance:	6km
Time:	2h50
Total ascent:	350m
Grade:	A
Start point:	Mourèze
Map:	IGN 2643 ouest (Lodève)

A walk which takes you through the dramatic Cirque de Mourèze and promises superb views on all sides – the surrounding hills, the coastal plain, the Pyrenees and the Lac du Salagou. It involves a fairly energetic climb up to the Mont Liausson ridge – flat once you're up there – and a nice, steady descent. Normally it is very peaceful, but avoid Sundays and Bank Holidays, as it is a favoured spot for French families with four-course picnics – guaranteed to make your ham sandwich look rather sad!

How to get there As for Walk 25.

The route Follow the route for Walk 25 through the **Cirque de Mourèze** until you come to the junction with the Anse and Gorges de Combasses path. Here, carry straight on, following red waymarks, and soon come to another sign, pointing you left, uphill; start a long, winding climb up to the **Mont Liausson ridge**. Towards the top, reach a horizontal crossing path and go left. Yellow waymarks join with the red here and guide you eventually over the ridge.

On reaching the ridge, walk a few metres north enjoy the view! The Lac du Salagou sits below you in all its glory with hills and more hills surrounding; note the dam at the right-hand end, the starting point for Walk 28. The path goes left and meanders along the ridge, soon passing the ruins of an old chapel. At the western end of the ridge is a large cairn. Behind it is a path which descends to the **Col de Portes**, where there is a junction of four paths. Go left (blue waymarks) towards **Mourèze**. From here, follow the instructions given in Walk 25 to get you back to your car.

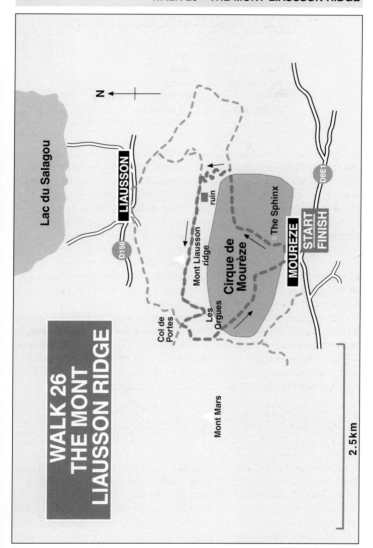

WALK 26
THE MONT
LIAUSSON RIDGE

Lac du Salagou

LIAUSSON

N

D156

Col de
Portes

Les
Orgues

Mont Liausson ridge

ruin

Cirque de
Mourèze

The Sphinx

MOURÈZE

START
FINISH

D8E1

Mont Mars

2.5km

Walk 27 – St Guilhem le Désert

Distance:	10km
Time:	3 hours
Total ascent:	500m
Grade:	B
Start point:	St Guilhem
Map:	IGN 2642 est (St Guilhem)

In the valley of the River Hérault, 40km northwest of Montpellier, St Guilhem le Désert is a beautiful, ancient village tucked tightly into a ravine beneath cliffs of tortured dolomitic rock. Despite being something of a tourist honeypot in the summer, it has retained its charm and is well worth a visit in its own right. The most striking building is that of the Abbaye de Gellone, a magnificent monastery founded in the year 800 by Guillaume de Toulouse, a companion of Charlemagne. However, this walk, which requires a reasonable level of fitness, will explore some of the wild country surrounding the village, particularly the stunning Cirque de l'Infernet. Part of the path follows the route taken by pilgrims heading for St Jacques de Compostelle in northern Spain. If you see someone with a scallop shell attached to their rucksack, they're a pilgrim.

If you are spending a few days in the area, a drive up the Hérault gorge will be rewarding. Visit the Grotte de Clamouse, just south of St Guilhem, and the Grotte des Demoiselles, south of Ganges. From Ganges, head west on the D25 down the Gorges de la Vis and visit the Cirque de Navacelles. Don't forget to try the local wines – Montpeyroux and St Saturnin produce some very fine AOC Coteaux du Languedoc!

How to get there From Gignac take the D32 to Aniane, then the D27, which meets the River Hérault and follows it up the gorge past the Grotte de Clamouse to St Guilhem. Go up to the car park at the top of the village.

The route From the car park, go left into the village square, shaded by an enormous plane tree. Find the Rue du Bout-du-Monde ('End of the world') at the far left corner of the square and follow it out of the village towards the valley of Verdus, picking up the red/white waymarks of a long-distance path. Cross the stream by a 'Feu interdit' ('No fires') sign. The path now zig-zags upwards through

An *arbousier* (strawberry tree)

Mushroom season –
but don't eat this one!

Blossom in mid-March

Heather in bloom

View across Lac du Salagou (Walk 29)

Narcissi by the path on Pic Saint-Baudille (Walk 29)

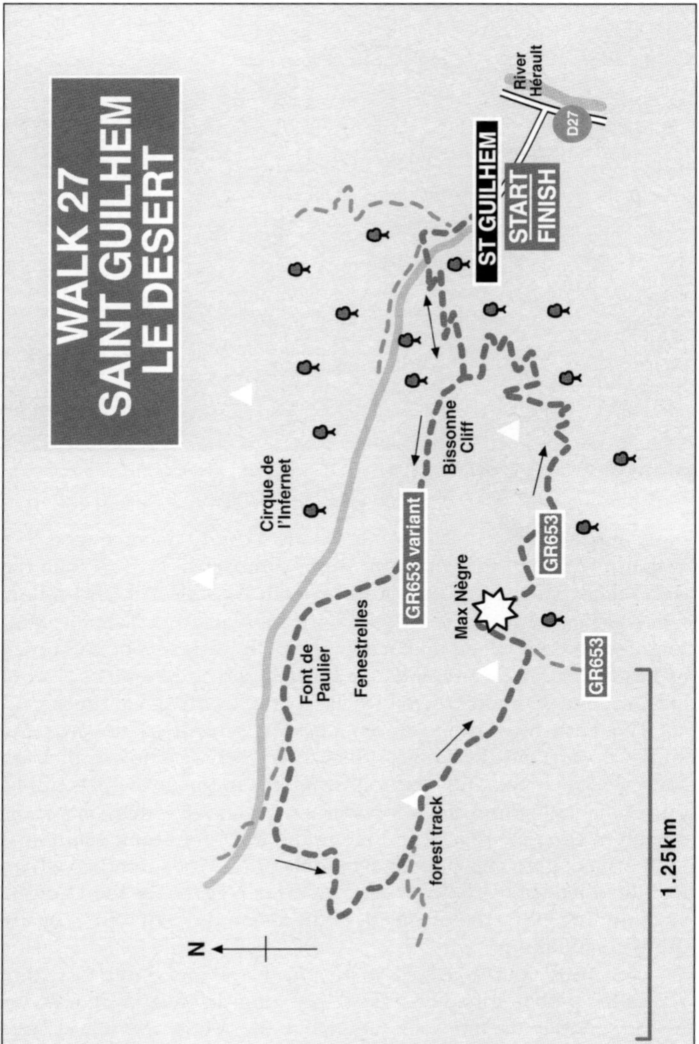

WALK 27
SAINT GUILHEM
LE DESERT

River
Hérault

D27

ST GUILHEM

START
FINISH

Cirque de
l'Infernet

GR653 variant

Bissonne
Cliff

GR653

Font de Paulier

Fenestrelles

Max Nègre

GR653

forest track

N

1.25km

Abbaye de Gellone, founded in 800AD at the ancient village of St Guilhem le Désert, is now home to a community of Carmelite nuns

pine, heather and *arbousier* for about 1km to meet a cliff (**La Bissonne**), where you may see some climbers in action. Take the right-hand path (GR653 variant) beneath the cliff face and follow what used to be the route by which the monks drove their sheep up to graze on the Plateau de Larzac. The path leads to a point known as **Les Fenestrelles**, a remarkable buttress which resembles a set of arcades; this was constructed by the monks in medieval times.

The path now drops down through pine trees towards the valley floor (Font de Paulier). Just after half way down, pick up some yellow waymarks and follow a path to the left which climbs out of the valley to reach a forest track. Head left – there is a short stretch of concrete road – and along the track for about 400m. Just after a small green metal post, where the track turns right, go left on a path which leads to a viewing area (**Max Nègre**).The views of the surrounding cliffs, the Cirque de l'Infernet and down to the sea are quite breathtaking.

Now head southeast back to the pine forest and down to a point where the path is joined on a bend by a long-distance path (GR653). Swing round to the left, soon seeing that the yellow waymarks have been joined by red/white marks; follow them eastwards to reach a balcony path with excellent views into the Cirque de l'Infernet. On a windy day, stay well back from the edge! The path then winds down through delightful pine forest back to **La Bissonne**. Here, go right and follow your original route back to **St Guilhem**.

Walk 28 – Lac du Salagou

Distance:	16km
Time:	5 hours
Total ascent:	200m
Grade:	A/B
Start point:	Lac du Salagou dam
Map:	IGN 2643 ouest (Lodève)

In the late 1960s a dam was built across the Salagou stream, giving birth to the vast Lac du Salagou. Although originally intended as an addition to the area's water supply, the lake's main function now is as a centre for leisure. Windsurfers, sailors, walkers, cyclists and fishermen can all find much to enjoy. For nature-lovers, birds and butterflies abound.

The landscape is extraordinary – to the south of the lake rises the Mont Liausson with its bright limestone outcrops; virtually every other view is dominated by the deep red, gritty soil of the ruffes – arid, easily eroded slopes on which vegetation has a precarious existence.

Our walk explores the northern shore of the lake and, from its high points, provides wonderful views across the water.

How to get there Take the D156 out of Clermont l'Hérault and the D156E to the dam (*barrage*). Park by the dam.

The route The entire walk is waymarked in yellow. Head down the tarmac road past the dam and wind down to ford the stream some 500m further on. Carry on along the road until you reach a left fork with a barrier across it. Don't be put off – go up this track until you reach a small **weather station** on your left. Take the first path on the right and wind gently uphill, ignoring all minor tracks. Go past the remains of an old quarry – enjoying the wonderful pillars of basalt

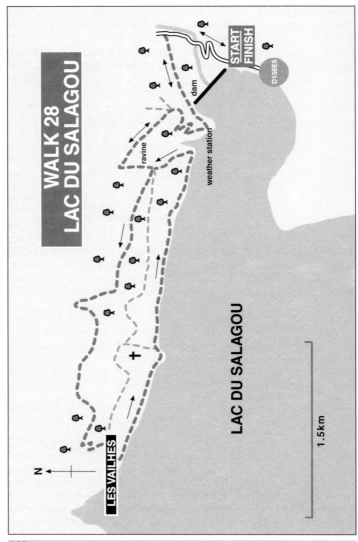

WALK 28
LAC DU SALAGOU

START
FINISH

D156E5

dam

weather station

ravine

LAC DU SALAGOU

1.5km

LES VAILHES

N

– then climb left through the evergreen oaks. At the top, turn left. The path joins a wider track; follow it to the left, round the edge of the ravine.

At a junction go right, and to the right of a forest road pick up a wide track with a barrier bearing the letters DFCI across it and follow it for about 3km. At a bend, descend to the left and soon arrive at the hamlet of **Les Vailhés**. (In summer there is a busy camp site here; for the rest of the year it is very quiet.) Go through the hamlet, past a *gîte* called La Maison du Lac and down to the lakeshore. Here is a perfect spot for a picnic; otherwise, go left and follow the shoreline. Where the cycle track (marked VTT) turns left to go up to a **chapel** (Notre Dame des Clans), continue straight along the shore of the lake. The path meanders a bit, so keep a look out for the yellow markings. Look out, too, for some interesting carvings sitting on a mound to your left. Shortly after two stone buildings, take the left-hand path, which climbs steeply up the ridge to a track. Go right and immediately come to a junction. Turn right and follow your outward footsteps back to the **dam**. (A notice tells you that you should not walk across the dam, but no-one seems to obey – you, your feet and your conscience must decide whether you take the short-cut across, or whether you continue round by the road!)

Walk 29 – Around Le Puech

Distance:	14km
Time:	4.5h
Total ascent:	250m
Grade:	A
Start point:	Le Puech
Map:	IGN 2643 ouest (Lodève)

A very pleasant walk in which you discover a little-known region between the Lac du Salagou and Lodève. The area is an extraordinary geological chaos: within a few yards the landscape can change from granite to schist to limestone, from ruffe (gritty red soil) to basalt to volcanic lava and back

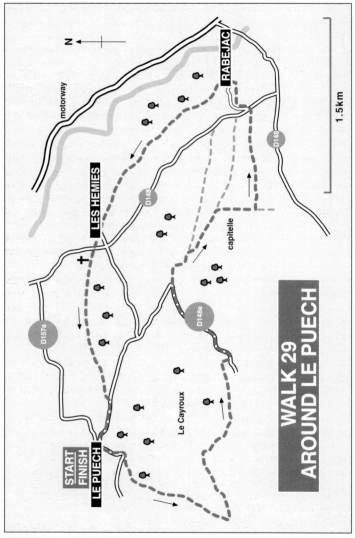

N ←

motorway

RABEJAC

1.5km

D148

LES HEMIES

D148

capitelle

D157e

D148e

Le Cayroux

WALK 29
AROUND LE PUECH

START
FINISH
LE PUECH

again. This walk takes us from the pretty hamlet of Le Puech up onto the plateau at the top of the hill known as Le Cayroux, from which there are long views in all directions. You will see a number of capitelles – the stone shelters built by shepherds to protect themselves from sun and storm.

How to get there From Bédarieux, take the D908 towards Clermont l'Hérault. Turn off left to Salasc, then go on to Octon. From there, follow signs towards Lodève, eventually coming to a left turn signed Le Puech (D148). On reaching the village, park close to the Mairie.

The route (The walk is very clearly waymarked at regular intervals in yellow.) From the metal cross in front of the Mairie, follow the road down to the right of the Mairie. After some 200m, on a bend in the road, a well-signed path goes off to the left and starts to climb gently up the side of the hill, opening out to give views across the valley. You will soon arrive without difficulty at a plateau. The path veers right and follows the edge of the plateau.

To the north you can see the cliffs of the Pas de l'Escalette, which have been drilled through to allow for the passage of the new A75 motorway between Clermont Ferrand and Montpellier.

At a dolmen the path goes left. Note the sudden change in the colour of the rocks and soil at this point. Follow the signposts up to the summit plateau of **Le Cayroux**. Here, you may find a great deal of disturbed soil, which is a sign that wild boar have been out during the night, snuffling for roots and other tasty treats. Fear not, they will be sleeping it off now!

As you cross the plateau, the view opens up to the south, with glimpses of the Lac du Salagou and the Mont Liausson (Walks 25 and 26). To the east you can see the Pic Saint-Baudille with its television transmitter on the top (Walk 30).

Go through a gap in a dry-stone wall and turn right. Shortly, go through another wall-gap and pass your first *capitelle*. At a clump of oak trees bear right then quickly left. The path starts to drop steadily downwards, with a view of the Lac du Salagou ahead. A less elevating sight is the motorway heading up towards Lodève. A convenient flat rock allows you to sit and look across to the lake. Note in the foreground the tortured shape of the *ruffes* which are so predominant in this valley.

From here the path descends steeply towards a road – take care, as the gritty soil can be unstable. At the road (**D148e**), bear left and follow it for about 800m. Ignore any yellow crosses which may be marked on the road and go past a house on your right, admiring the enormous outdoor dining-table! Carry on along the road until you come to a left-hand bend. Here, a sign-post tells you to bear right onto a broad, rocky path. You are now walking through the middle of an area of *ruffes*. At a junction with a downward left-hand track, go straight on for some 250m. Look carefully for a path going off to the right and follow it. Pass a ruined *capitelle* after about 40m and soon come to a much larger one, which is well worth a look inside. It is beautifully made. Note how the interior wall slopes gradually inwards to give a 'bee-hive' effect; also enjoy the coolness of the interior – very welcome on a hot day!

With your back to the entrance of the *capitelle*, go straight ahead and slightly downwards. A small house and vineyard come into view. Cross the bed of a stream and walk up through the vineyard to the house. Go to the left of the house and join the drive which bears away to the left, leaving the yellow waymarks temporarily. Follow the drive for about 800m, picking up the waymarks again, until you reach a road. Cross the road and take the narrow road opposite, signed '**Rabejac**'. Walk through the hamlet, and as you emerge at the far end turn 90 degrees left and walk down towards a large modern barn. A yellow waymark on the left-hand end of the barn directs you along a cement road to the right of a tarmac sports area. Turn left off the road along a grassy track. In front of you is the hill of Le Cayroux, which you explored earlier.

Cross the bed of a stream and bear right towards a wooden electricity pole. The upward track is broad, red and rocky. It climbs steadily up for some 250m through a fragrant mix of cistus, juniper, green oak and bush heather to a junction on a ridge. Just when you thought you were lost in the Mediterranean *garrigue*, here you are confronted with a motorway and a rather disgusting little industrial estate! Turn your back on that and concentrate instead on the view back down the path and across to the Lac du Salagou and the Mont Liausson.

Turn left along a broad ridge track. After 600m, reach a junction and take the right-hand path. At the next junction, fork right and downhill to the hamlet of **Les Hémies**. Walk through the hamlet and, opposite a house with an odd gabled front entrance, go right along a narrow, partially-covered lane. The path bears left between stone walls and goes between meadows to reach a road.

Cross the road and climb up the path opposite. At the top, go left, then soon right on a broad track. To the north, beyond some greenhouses, the tower of Lodève Cathedral can be seen nestling between the hills. Pass the ruins of the **Chapelle Saint-Agricole** and climb gently to an electricity pylon. Pass to the left of this and on to another metal excrescence at the top of the hill. Then start to descend, with the hill of Le Cayroux ahead. A lovely view of **Le Puech** opens up to the right.

Drop down to the road, turn right, and at an electricity pylon take a narrow path off to the right which leads you back to the village.

Walk 30 – Pic Saint-Baudille

Distance:	9km
Time:	3h30
Total ascent:	450m
Grade:	A/B
Start point:	**La Font du Griffe**
Map:	**IGN 2642 est (St Guilhem le Désert)**

At nearly 850m, the Pic Saint-Baudille is the highest peak in the range known as the Montagnes de la Séranne, which lead gently northeast from the plain to the Cévennes. The limestone outcrop which tops the peak is crowned by a transmitter station handling signals for all France's terrestrial television channels as well as radio.

The walk is quite straightforward and well waymarked, with a steady uphill section and a gentle descent, apart from one short steep section in both. The views from Pic Saint-Baudille are absolutely breathtaking – to the south, a huge panorama of the Mediterranean plain, the coastline of the entire Golfe du Lion, from Montpellier to the Spanish border, the Pyrenees; to the north, the Cévennes and even, on a clear spring morning, the Mont Blanc! Further on, as you descend towards the start point, look across to the Cirque de l'Infernet and the La Bissonne described in Walk 27. A great

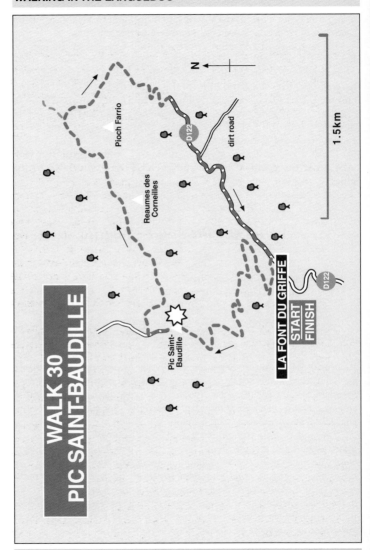

WALK 30
PIC SAINT-BAUDILLE

Pic Saint-Baudille

Pioch Farrio

Reaumes des Corneilles

D122

dirt road

N

1.5km

LA FONT DU GRIFFE
START
FINISH

D122

day out. Take some sunglasses, though – the glare of bright sunshine on white limestone can be painful if you aren't used to it!

How to get there From Clermont l'Hérault, take the N9 north. Turn off right to Ceyras and take the D141 north to St Félix de Lodez. From there, head for St Saturnin and on to Arboras. Just before you enter Arboras, turn right on to the D9, signed Montpeyroux. Very soon, go left on the D122, signed St Jean de Buèges. This very exciting single-track road takes you to the foot of Saint-Baudille at La Font du Griffe, where there is a goat farm. There is a small car park opposite the buildings.

The route Walk a few metres up the road. On the left is a small, square transformer station. The path goes up behind this (red/white waymarks) and heads gently uphill behind the goat farm. After some 250m, on a bend, a path goes sharply off to the right (an old wooden board rather blearily signs 'St-Baudille') and climbs steadily up through white limestone rock, stunted evergreen oaks and cistus. It is not long before the view to the south opens up. In the foreground are the vines of Montpeyroux and Saint-Saturnin, both highly reputed for their wines. To the southwest are Mont Liausson and the Pic de Vissou (Walks 25 and 26), and to the east is the unmistakeable shark's-fin outline of the Pic St Loup, north of Montpellier.

The summit of **Saint-Baudille** soon comes into view, with its red and white antenna. After a series of hairpin bends, you arrive at the airy Col de la Mulatière and can look northwards to the Cévennes. Ignore a right-hand descending path and point yourself in the direction of the antenna. Follow the path 90 degrees right which sets off up the ridge. As you approach the antenna and its compound, the path veers round to the back left-hand corner of the compound and emerges (rather disappointingly after all that effort) onto a tarmac road. Turn right up the road and go up a track to the left of the compound, signed 'Table d'Orientation' (**viewing platform**). A ceramic table on the platform shows you all that there is to see on a clear day, and it is a vast panorama, well worth a dawn start so as to avoid the inevitable heat-haze on sunny days.

Retrace your steps back to the road and follow it for about 100m to turn right onto a track which crosses a small parking area. From this point, waymarking is yellow. Go on past a grassy plateau and through some rusty gateposts. The obvious track ascends gently and veers northeast below the summit of a hill called **Beaumes des Corneilles**, giving excellent views towards the Cirque de Navacelles and Le Caylar (see Walk 31). Pass some 80m to the left of a small antenna, and ahead of you see the summit of the **Pioch Farrio**. Our walk will take us round below the summit of Farrio and down the eastern slope. Soon, the path turns eastwards and descends to a broad col by a wire fence. Just before it starts to climb again, look for a path 90 degrees right (yellow waymark). This takes you gently downhill above a ravine, with lovely views across to the Pic St Loup and the sea.

As the path turns away from the ravine, heading south, look across to the great rocky outcrop of La Bissonne cliff above St Guilhem (Walk 27). The descent is long and steady, easy on the legs, until the last 100m, where it drops steeply through tall broom to a road. Turn right onto the road (D122) and follow it for about 2km back to the goat farm at **La Font du Griffe**. Some road-walking can be a bore – not this!

Walk 31 – Le Caylar and La Couvertoirade

Distance:	17.5km
Time:	5 hours
Total ascent:	120m
Grade:	B
Start point:	Le Caylar
Map:	IGN 2642 ouest

A very different walk from all the others, in that it is almost flat. It starts at an altitude of 720m and never goes higher than 790m. After a steady, longish ramble, easy well-marked paths lead across part of the wild, lonely Causse du Larzac, the largest of the causses (limestone plateaux) in the region. The causse is used heavily for sheep-grazing, and between spring and autumn you are likely to see large flocks up there, all producing milk to make Roquefort cheese.

There is history too – in the 12th century, the Order of the Knights

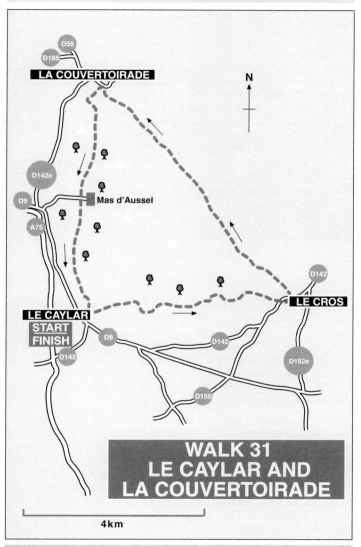

WALK 31
LE CAYLAR AND
LA COUVERTOIRADE

4km

The ancient fortified town of La Couvertoirade, once the property of the Knights Templar

Templar was given part of the Causse du Larzac. A local headquarters was built at Sainte-Eulalie-de-Cernon, with annexes at La Cavalerie and La Couvertoirade. In the early 14th century, these were taken over by the Knights of St John of Jerusalem. Our walk takes us to the fortified town of La Couvertoirade, where you can spend a delightful half-hour or so wandering the ancient streets.

Take an extra layer of clothing – it is not the Mediterranean plain up here, and the wind can be very cold.

How to get there There is a wonderful drive up from Bédarieux: take the D35 Lodève road to Lunas. At a junction on top of the hill beyond Lunas, take the D142 all the way to Le Caylar, enjoying fabulous views across the Escandorgue hills and the Monts d'Orb. Alternatively, take the N9 out of Clermont l'Hérault, which joins the A75 motorway, go through the tunnel of the Pas de l'Escalette and come off at Le Caylar. Park in the village square by a tree which has been magnificently carved by a local wood sculptor, showing features of local life.

The route From the tree, with the tourist office in front of you, walk to the right along Rue du Quai, on into the Rue de l'Eglise and then bear left into the Rue du Camp Laurier. As you leave the village, pass a football pitch on your right to reach a round pond known as a *lavogne*. These *lavognes* are very common in the area. They are man-made ponds which store rainwater for the benefit of thirsty sheep. You will see an excellent example just outside the walls of La Couvertoirade.

Turn right between the pitch and the pond to join a broad track with yellow waymarks. This will take you all the way to the village of Le Cros, 3.5km away. All around you is the light grey, dolomitic rock which dominates the *causse*, often in the form of huge, jutting boulders, dry-stone walls or just in loose piles. The trees are thickly covered in pale green lichen. After about 1.5km the path narrows to go between lines of cistus. A view to the north opens up and, half-left, the hills of the Cévennes can be seen.

The track soon broadens again and passes to the right of a farmhouse, becoming an unmetalled road. A further 800m brings you in sight of the compact little village of **Le Cros**. Drop down to a road, turn left and enter the village. At the centre of the village is a junction of roads, and a lovely old post-box on the wall ahead. Take the road to the left of the post-box, passing the portcullis-like gate of the château. In front of you is a building with a clock and bell. Turn left down a lane, following the high wall of the *château* and leave the village, now following yellow/red waymarks. Pass a lovely stone cross and follow the broad unmetalled road out onto the *causse*. Soon you can look across to the left and see the great rock beneath which nestles the village of Le Caylar.

Le Cros to La Couvertoirade is about 8km. The track is exposed to the elements, with very little possibility of shade from the sun or shelter from the wind. It feels very isolated, especially when the sheep are not up there. A description of the features of the *causse* – rock, scrubland, stunted trees – does not do the place justice. Like many of the uplands of Britain, it has a special feel about it which encourages the walker to appreciate the surroundings while, at the same time, indulging in exquisite daydreams!

The track forks close to a round pond (have a peep at the goldfish). Bear right here. As you move further into the *causse*, the grazing areas on either side of the track become more prominent.

An unusual disc-shaped gravestone in the village cemetery at Couvertoirade

Look out for the large, beige-coloured thistle-heads that grow amongst the grasses. These are known locally as *cardabelles* and are very much a part of the culture of the area. They are often seen nailed to the front door of local houses and are meant to protect the home from harm; they also act as a barometer. The sun-shaped heart of the plant closes up when the atmosphere is damp and opens in dry weather.

The well-waymarked track winds on through this wonderful desolation until suddenly, as you round a bend, the walls and towers of **La Couvertoirade** come into view. Drop down to the village, passing a superb *lavogne* by the south entrance (Portal d'Aval). Enter the fortified village (you may have to pay during the tourist season) and explore the delightful old streets within the walls. Very few people live there now, but there are some little shops selling pottery, and the like, and a café/restaurant. Do have a look in the church and the graveyard next to it.

Retrace your steps to the Portal d'Aval. Immediately opposite this gate is a grassy track between two stone walls. This is the GR71b long-distance path, with red/white waymarks. It will take you back to Le Caylar, 6km away. The path winds between some meadows initially, then heads gently uphill. When it meets a crossing-path, turn left and follow the narrow path between cistus bushes.

There is no difficulty in following the track; it is clearly and regularly marked, so relax and enjoy the views across the *causse*. Eventually, the austere buildings of the **Mas d'Aussel** (a large farmhouse and barn) appear ahead. Take care at this point to take a right fork just before a grassy meadow in front of the property. There is a small notice in a tree at this fork which says: 'Amis randonneurs, respectez la propriété privée' ('Keep out!'). Bear to the right of the notice and enter a narrow path with a hedge on your left and cultivated fields on your right. Follow this to the farm road, cross the road and enter another lane which passes to the right of the farm.

Carry on southwards, with the rock of Le Caylar ahead, topped with a cross. Faint rumblings from the A75 motorway can be heard in the distance. As you approach **Le Caylar**, the terrain on either side of the path becomes rockier and quite spectacular. Dry-stone walls appear alongside, thickly covered in shaggy, bright green moss. At times you are hemmed in by huge overhanging rocks.

Reach a crossing path with a sign. Go left and soon bear right, starting to climb up into the rocky mound ahead. The path skirts at mid-height round the left-hand side of the mound (passing a wooden sculpture trail which you can explore, energy permitting) then drops down to a road. Turn right to enter the village.

ENGLISH–FRENCH GLOSSARY

Hello!	salut!, bonjour!
Good evening	bonsoir
Good night	bonne nuit
Goodbye	au revoir
Yes/no	oui/non
Please	s'il vous plaît
Thank you (very much)	merci (beaucoup)
I'm English	Je suis Anglais
I don't speak French	Je ne parle pas français
Do you speak English?	Parlez-vous anglais?
Is there a bakery near here?	Est-ce qu'il y a une boulangerie près d'ici ?
Where is the bank, please?	Où est la banque, s'il vous plaît?
The market/the toilets/ the station	le marché/les toilettes/la gare
Excuse me…	Pardon, monsieur/madame/ mademoiselle…
Petrol station	station-service
Unleaded	sans plomb
Turn left/right	tournez à gauche/à droite
Go straight on	allez tout droit
How much is this?	C'est combien?
Do you have a room, please?	Avez-vous une chambre, s'il vous plaît ?
For two people	pour deux personnes
With shower/bathroom	avec douche/salle de bains
Double bed/single bed	grand lit/lit pour une personne
For one night	pour une nuit
(White) coffee	café (au lait **or** grand'crème)
Tea (with milk/lemon)	thé (au lait/au citron)

A carafe of red/white/rosé	une carafe **or** un pichet de rouge/blanc/rosé
Mineral water	eau minérale
(Draught) beer	bière (pression)
Orange juice	jus d'orange
Dish of the day	plat du jour
Ice cream	glace
The bill, please!	L'addition, s'il vous plait!
Footpath	sentier
Track	chemin
Waymarking	balisage
Hunting/hunter	la chasse/le chasseur
I'm lost!	Je suis perdu!

SUMMARY OF
WALKS

CICERONE GUIDES

WALKING AND TREKKING IN THE ALPS

WALKING IN THE ALPS *Kev Reynolds* The popular author of many of our Alpine guide-books now draws on his vast experience to produce an outstanding comprehensive volume. Every area covered. Not for over half a century has there been anything remotely comparable. Fully illustrated. *ISBN 1 85284 261 X Large format Case bound 496pp*
CHAMONIX TO ZERMATT - The Walker's Haute Route *Kev Reynolds* The classic walk in the shadow of great peaks from Mont Blanc to the Matterhorn. In 14 stages, this is one of the most beautiful LD paths in Europe. *ISBN 1 85284 215 6 176pp*
THE GRAND TOUR OF MONTE ROSA *C.J. Wright*
Vol 1: - MARTIGNY TO VALLE DELLA SESIA (via the Italian valleys) *ISBN 1 85284 177 X 216pp*
Vol 2: - VALLE DELLA SESIA TO MARTIGNY (via the Swiss valleys) *ISBN 1 85284 178 8 182pp* The ultimate alpine LD walk which encircles most of the Pennine Alps.
TOUR OF MONT BLANC *Andrew Harper* One of the world's best walks - the circum-navigation of the Mont Blanc massif. 120 miles of pure magic, split into 11 sections. Reprinted and updated. *ISBN 1 85284 240 7 144pp PVC cover*
100 HUT WALKS IN THE ALPS *Kev Reynolds* 100 walks amid dramatic mountain scenery to high mountain huts, each with a map, photograph and route description. A fine introduction to Europe's highest mountains in France, Italy, Switzerland, Austria and Slovenia. *ISBN 1 85284 297 0*

FRANCE, BELGIUM AND LUXEMBOURG

WALKING IN THE ARDENNES *Alan Castle* 53 circular walks in this attractive area of gorges and deep cut wooded valleys, caves, castles and hundreds of walking trails. Easily accessible from the channel. *ISBN 1 85284 213 X 224pp*
SELECTED ROCK CLIMBS IN BELGIUM AND LUXEMBOURG *Chris Craggs* Perfect rock, good protection and not too hot to climb in summer. *ISBN 1 85284 155 9 188p A5*
THE BRITTANY COASTAL PATH *Alan Castle* The GR34, 360 miles, takes a month to walk. Easy access from UK means it can be split into several holidays. *ISBN 1 85284 185 0 296pp*
CHAMONIX - MONT BLANC - A Walking Guide *Martin Collins* In the dominating presence of Europe's highest mountain, the scenery is exceptional. A comprehensive guide to the area. *ISBN 1 85284 009 9 192pp PVC cover*
THE CORSICAN HIGH LEVEL ROUTE - Walking the GR20 *Alan Castle* The most challenging of the French LD paths - across the rocky spine of Corsica. *ISBN 1 85284 100 1 TOP New edition expected autumn 2000*
WALKING THE FRENCH ALPS: GR5 *Martin Collins* The popular trail from Lake Geneva to Nice. Split into stages, each of which could form the basis of a good holiday. *ISBN 1 85284 051 X 160pp*
WALKING IN THE FRENCH GORGES *Alan Castle* 320 miles through Provence and Ardèche, includes the famous gorges of the Verdon. *ISBN 1 85284 114 1 224pp*
FRENCH ROCK *Bill Birkett* THE guide to many exciting French crags! Masses of photo topos, with selected hit-routes in detail. *ISBN 1 85284 113 3. 332pp A5 size*
WALKING IN THE HAUTE SAVOIE *Janette Norton* 61 walks in the pre-Alps of Chablais, to majestic peaks in the Faucigny, Haut Giffre and Lake Annecy regions. *ISBN 1 85284 196 6 312pp*

TOUR OF THE OISANS: GR54 *Andrew Harper* This popular walk around the Dauphiné massif and Écrins national park is similar in quality to the celebrated Tour of Mont Blanc. A two week suggested itinerary covers the 270km route. *ISBN 1 85284 157 5   120pp PVC cover*

TOUR OF MONT BLANC *see Walking and Trekking in the Alps, above*

WALKING IN PROVENCE   *Janette Norton* 42 walks through the great variety of Provence - remote plateaux, leafy gorges, ancient villages, monuments, quiet towns. Provence is evocative of a gentler life. *ISBN 1 85284 293 8 248pp*

THE PYRENEAN TRAIL: GR10 *Alan Castle* From the Atlantic to the Mediterranean at a lower level than the Pyrenean High Route. 50 days but splits into holiday sections.   *ISBN 1 85284 245 8 176pp*

WALKS AND CLIMBS IN THE PYRENEES *Kev Reynolds   See entry under FRANCE/SPAIN*

THE TOUR OF THE QUEYRAS *Alan Castle* A 13 day walk which traverses wild but beautiful country, the sunniest part of the French Alps. Suitable for a first Alpine visit. *ISBN 1 85284 048 X   160pp*

THE ROBERT LOUIS STEVENSON TRAIL *Alan Castle* 140 mile trail in the footsteps of Stevenson's *Travels with a Donkey* through the Cevennes, from Le Puy to St Jean du Gard. This route is ideal for people new to walking holidays. *ISBN 1 85284 060 9 160pp*

ROCK CLIMBS IN THE PYRENEES *Derek Walker See entry under FRANCE/SPAIN*

WALKING IN THE TARENTAISE AND BEAUFORTAIN ALPS *J.W. Akitt* The delectable mountain area south of Mont Blanc includes the Vanoise National Park. 53 day walks, 5 tours between 2 and 8 day's duration, plus 40 short outings. *ISBN 1 85284 181 8 216pp*

ROCK CLIMBS IN THE VERDON - An Introduction *Rick Newcombe* An English-style guide, which makes for easier identification of the routes and descents.   *ISBN 1 85284 015 3   72pp*

TOUR OF THE VANOISE   *Kev Reynolds* A 10-12 day circuit of one of the finest mountain areas of France, between Mt. Blanc and the Écrins. The second most popular mountain tour after the Tour of Mont Blanc.   *ISBN 1 85284 224 5   120pp*

WALKS IN VOLCANO COUNTRY *Alan Castle* Two LD walks in Central France, the High Auvergne and Tour of the Velay, in a unique landscape of extinct volcanoes. *ISBN 1 85284 092 7 208pp*

THE WAY OF ST JAMES *Two titles - see below*

FRANCE/SPAIN

ROCK CLIMBS IN THE PYRENEES *Derek Walker* Includes Pic du Midi d'Ossau and the Vignemale in France, and the Ordesa Canyon and Riglos in Spain. *ISBN 1 85284 039 0 168pp PVC cover*

WALKS AND CLIMBS IN THE PYRENEES *Kev Reynolds* Includes the Pyrenean High Level Route. Invaluable for any backpacker or mountaineer who plans to visit this still unspoilt mountain range. (3rd Edition)   *ISBN 1 85284 133 8 328pp   PVC cover*

THE WAY OF ST JAMES: Le Puy to Santiago - A Cyclist's Guide *John Higginson* A guide for touring cyclists follows as closely as possible the original route but avoids the almost unrideable sections of the walkers' way. On surfaced lanes and roads. *ISBN 1 85284 274 1 112pp*

THE WAY OF ST JAMES: Le Puy to Santiago - A Walker's Guide *Alison Raju* A walker's guide to the ancient route of pilgrimage. Plus the continuation to Finisterre. *ISBN 1 85284 271 7 264pp*

SPAIN AND PORTUGAL

WALKING IN THE ALGARVE *June Parker* The author of *Walking in Mallorca* turns her expert attention to the Algarve, with a selection of walks to help the visitor explore the true countryside. *ISBN 1 85284 173 7 168pp*

ANDALUSIAN ROCK CLIMBS *Chris Craggs* El Chorro and El Torcal are world famous. Includes Tenerife. *ISBN 1 85284 109 5 168pp*

COSTA BLANCA ROCK *Chris Craggs* Over 1500 routes on over 40 crags, many for the first time in English. The most comprehensive guide to the area. *ISBN 1 85284 241 5 264pp*

MOUNTAIN WALKS ON THE COSTA BLANCA *Bob Stansfield* An easily accessible winter walking paradise to rival Mallorca. With rugged limestone peaks and warm climate. This guide includes the 150 km Costa Blanca Mountain Way. *ISBN1 85284 165 232pp*

ROCK CLIMBS IN MAJORCA, IBIZA AND TENERIFE *Chris Craggs* Holiday island cragging at its best. *ISBN 1 85284 189 3 240pp*

WALKING IN MALLORCA *June Parker.* The 3rd edition of this great classic guide, takes account of rapidly changing conditions. Revised reprint for 1999. *ISBN 1 85284 250 4 288pp PVC cover*

BIRDWATCHING IN MALLORCA *Ken Stoba* A complete guide to what to see and where to see it. *ISBN 1 85284 053 6 108pp*

THE MOUNTAINS OF CENTRAL SPAIN *Jaqueline Oglesby* Walks and scrambles in the Sierras de Gredos and Guadarrama which rise to 2600m and remain snow capped for 5 months of the year. *ISBN 1 85284 203 2 312pp*

ROCK CLIMBS IN THE PYRENEES *Derek Walker See entry under FRANCE/SPAIN*

THROUGH THE SPANISH PYRENEES: GR11 *Paul Lucia* An updated new edition of the long distance trail which mirrors the French GR10 but traverses much lonelier, wilder country. With new maps and information. *ISBN 1 85284 307 1 232pp*

WALKING IN THE SIERRA NEVADA *Andy Walmsley* Spain's highest mountain range is a wonderland for the traveller and wilderness backpacker alike. Mountain bike routes indicated. *ISBN 1 85284 194 X 160pp*

WALKS AND CLIMBS IN THE PICOS DE EUROPA *Robin Walker* A definitive guide to these unique mountains. Walks and rock climbs of all grades. *ISBN 1 85284 033 1 232pp PVC cover*

SWITZERLAND - including parts of France and Italy

ALPINE PASS ROUTE, SWITZERLAND *Kev Reynolds* Over 15 passes along the north ern edge of the Alps, past the Eiger, Jungfrau and many other renowned peaks. A 325 km route in 15 suggested stages. *ISBN 1 85284 069 2 176pp*

THE BERNESE ALPS, SWITZERLAND *Kev Reynolds* Walks around Grindelwald, Lauterbrunnen and Kandersteg dominated by the great peaks of the Oberland. *ISBN 1 85284 243 1 248pp PVC cover*

CENTRAL SWITZERLAND - A Walking Guide *Kev Reynolds* A little known but delightful area stretching from Luzern to the St Gotthard, includes Engelberg and Klausen Pass. *ISBN 1 85284 131 1 216pp PVC cover*

CHAMONIX TO ZERMATT — *see entry under Walking and Trekking in the Alps*

THE GRAND TOUR OF MONTE ROSA Vols 1 & 2 *See entry under Walking and Trekking in the Alps*

WALKS IN THE ENGADINE, SWITZERLAND *Kev Reynolds* The superb region to the south-east of Switzerland of the Bregaglia, Bernina Alps, and the Engadine National Park. *ISBN 1 85284 003 X 192pp PVC cover*

THE JURA: WALKING THE HIGH ROUTE *Kev Reynolds and* **WINTER SKI TRAVERSES** *R. Brian Evans.* The High Route is a long distance path along the highest crest of the Swiss Jura. In winter it is a paradise for cross-country skiers. Both sections in one volume.
ISBN 1 85284 010 2 192pp

WALKING IN TICINO, SWITZERLAND *Kev Reynolds* Walks in the lovely Italian part of Switzerland, little known to British walkers. *ISBN 1 85284 098 6 184pp PVC cover*
THE VALAIS, SWITZERLAND - A Walking Guide *Kev Reynolds* The splendid scenery of the Pennine Alps, with such peaks as the Matterhorn, Dent Blanche, and Mont Rosa providing a perfect background. *ISBN 1 85284 151 6 224pp PVC cover*

GERMANY, AUSTRIA AND EASTERN EUROPE

MOUNTAIN WALKING IN AUSTRIA *Cecil Davies* An enlarged second edition. 25 mountain groups, 98 walks from half a day to a good week. *ISBN 1 85284 239 3 126pp*
WALKING IN THE BAVARIAN ALPS *Grant Bourne & Sabine Korner-Bourne* 57 walks of variety in the Allgau, Ammergau, Wetterstein, Tegernsee, Chiemgau and Berchtesgarden Alps on the German-Austrian border. *ISBN 1 85284 229 6 184pp*
WALKING IN THE BLACK FOREST *Fleur & Colin Speakman* Above the Rhine valley, the Ortenauer Wine path (64km) and the Clock Carriers Way (10 day circular walk) are described, together with practical walking advice for the area in general. *ISBN 1 85284 050 1 120p*
GERMANY'S ROMANTIC ROAD A Guide for Walkers and Cyclists *Gordon McLachlan* 423km past historic walled towns and castles of southern Germany. *ISBN 1 85284 233 4 208pp*
WALKING IN THE HARZ MOUNTAINS *Fleur & Colin Speakman* 30 walks in Germany's most northerly mountains, some from the narrow gauge steam railway. *ISBN 1 85284 149 4 152pp*
KING LUDWIG WAY *Fleur and Colin Speakman* Travels the Bavarian countryside from Munich to Füssen. King Ludwig was responsible for the fabulous castle of Neuschwanstein and sponsored Wagner's operas. *ISBN 0 902363 90 5 80pp*
KLETTERSTEIG - Scrambles in the Northern Limestone Alps *Paul Werner Translated by Dieter Pevsner* Protected climbing paths similar to the Via Ferrata in the German/Austrian border region. *ISBN 0 902363 46 8 184pp PVC cover*
THE MOUNTAINS OF ROMANIA *James Roberts* A definitive guide to the newly accessible Carpathian mountains. Potentially one of the best walking destinations in Europe, with mountain wilderness and friendly people. *ISBN 1 85284 295 4 296pp*
WALKING THE RIVER RHINE TRAIL *Alan Castle* A spectacular 170mile (273km) walk along Germany's most famous river from Bonn to Alsheim near Worms. Excellent public transport assists the walker. *ISBN 1 85284 276 8 176pp*
WALKING IN THE SALZKAMMERGUT *Fleur and Colin Speakman* Holiday rambles in Austria's Lake District. Renowned for its historic salt mines. *ISBN 1 85284 030 7 104pp*
HUT TO HUT IN THE STUBAI ALPS *Allan Hartley* The Stubai Rucksack Route and The Stubai Glacier Tour, each around 10 days. Easy peaks and good huts make it a good area for a first Alpine season. *ISBN 1 85284 123 0 128pp*
THE HIGH TATRAS *Colin Saunders & Renata Narozna* A detailed guide to the Tatras, popular area between Poland and Slovakia. *ISBN 1 85284 150 8 248pp PVC cover*

SCANDINAVIA

WALKING IN NORWAY *Constance Roos* 20 walking routes in the main mountain areas from the far south to the sub-arctic regions, all accessible by public transport. *ISBN 1 85284 230 X 200pp*

ITALY AND SLOVENIA

ALTA VIA - HIGH LEVEL WALKS IN THE DOLOMITES *Martin Collins* A guide to some of the most popular mountain paths in Europe - Alta Via 1 and 2. *ISBN 0 902363 75 1 160pp PVC cover*

THE CENTRAL APENNINES OF ITALY - Walks, Scrambles and Climbs *Stephen Fox* The mountainous spine of Italy, with secluded walks, rock climbs and scrambles on the Gran Sasso d'Italia and some of Italy's finest sport climbing crags. *ISBN 1 85284 219 9 152pp*

WALKING IN THE CENTRAL ITALIAN ALPS *Gillian Price* The Vinschgau, Ortler and Adamello regions. Little known to British walkers, certain to become popular. *ISBN 1 85284 183 4 230pp PVC cover*

WALKING IN THE DOLOMITES *Gillian Price* A comprehensive selection of walks amongst spectacular rock scenery. By far the best English guide to the area. *ISBN 1 85284 079 X PVC cover*

WALKING IN ITALY'S GRAN PARADISO *Gillian Price* Rugged mountains and desolate valleys with a huge variety of wildlife. Walks from short strolls to full-scale traverses. *ISBN 1 85284 231 8 200pp*

LONG DISTANCE WALKS IN THE GRAN PARADISO *J.W. Akitt* Includes Southern Valdotain. Supplements our Gran Paradiso guide by Gillian Price. Describes Alta Via 2 and the Grand Traverse of Gran Paradiso and some shorter walks. *ISBN 1 85284 247 4 168pp*

THE GRAND TOUR OF MONTE ROSA *C.J. Wright*
See entry under Walking and Trekking in the Alps

ITALIAN ROCK - Selected Climbs in Northern Italy *Al Churcher*. Val d'Orco and Mello, Lecco and Finale etc. A good introduction to some great crags. *ISBN 0 902363 93 X 200pp PVC cover*

WALKS IN THE JULIAN ALPS *Simon Brown* Slovenia contains some of Europe's most attractive mountain limestone scenery. 30 walks as an introduction to the area, from valley strolls to high mountain scrambles. *ISBN 1 85284 125 7 184pp*

WALKING IN TUSCANY *Gillian Price* 50 itineraries from brief strolls to multi-day treks in Tuscany, Umbria and Latium. *ISBN 1 85284 268 7 312pp*

VIA FERRATA SCRAMBLES IN THE DOLOMITES *Höfler/Werner Translated by Cecil Davies* The most exciting walks in the world. Wires, stemples and ladders enable the 'walker' to enter the climber's vertical environment. *ISBN 1 85284 089 7 248pp PVC cover*

OTHER MEDITERRANEAN COUNTRIES

THE ATLAS MOUNTAINS *Karl Smith* Trekking in the mountains of north Africa. Practical and comprehensive. *ISBN 1 85284 258 X 136pp PVC cover*

WALKING IN CYPRUS *Donald Brown* Without a guide getting lost in Cyprus is easy. Donald Brown shares undiscovered Cyprus with 26 easy to moderate routes for walkers. *ISBN 1 85284 195 8 144pp*

THE MOUNTAINS OF GREECE - A Walker's Guide *Tim Salmon* Hikes of all grades from a month-long traverse of the Pindos to day hikes on the outskirts of Athens. *ISBN 1 85284 108 7 PVC cover*

CRETE - THE WHITE MOUNTAINS *Loraine Wilson* Describes 49 walks graded from modest to demanding, in this spectacularly beautiful range of mountains in the west of Crete. Includes Samaria gorge, high mountains up to 2500 metres, and glorious coastal walks. *ISBN 1 85284 298 9 152pp*

THE MOUNTAINS OF TURKEY *Karl Smith* Over 100 treks and scrambles with detailed route descriptions of all the popular peaks. Includes Ararat. *ISBN 1 85284 161 3 184pp PVC cover*

TREKS AND CLIMBS IN WADI RUM, JORDAN *Tony Howard* The world's foremost desert climbing and trekking area. Increasingly popular every year as word of its quality spreads. *ISBN 1 85284 254 7 252pp A5 Card cover*

JORDAN - Walks, Treks, Caves, Climbs, Canyons in Pella, Ajlun, Moab, Dana, Petra and Rum *Di Taylor & Tony Howard* The first guidebook to the superlative routes found in Jordan's recently formed Nature Reserves. These are walks, treks, caves and climbs described in this little known landscape by the authors of our Wadi Rum guide. *ISBN 1 85284 278 4 192pp A5*

THE ALA DAG, Climbs and Treks in Turkey's Crimson Mountains *O.B. Tüzel* The best mountaineering area in Turkey. *ISBN 1 85284 112 5 296pp PVC cover*

HIMALAYA

ADVENTURE TREKS IN NEPAL *Bill O'Connor*
ISBN 1 85223 306 0 160pp large format

ANNAPURNA - A Trekker's Guide *Kev Reynolds* Includes Annapurna Circuit, the Annapurna Santuary and the Pilgrim's Trail, with lots of good advice. *ISBN 1 85284 132 X 184pp*

EVEREST - A Trekker's Guide *Kev Reynolds* A new second edition of this guide to the most popular trekking region in the Himalaya. Lodges, tea-house, permits, health - all are dealt with in this indispensible guide. With updated information, clear mapping and superb photography, including detailed descriptions of approach routes from both Nepal and Tibet. *ISBN 1 85284 306 3 184pp*

GARHWAL AND KUMAON - A Trekker's and Visitor's Guide *K.P.Sharma* Almost at the centre of the Himalayan chain culminating in Nanda Devi. Garhwal consists of rugged mountains and valleys, Kumaon is more gentle. *ISBN 1 85284 264 4 200pp*

KANGCHENJUNGA - A Trekker's Guide *Kev Reynolds* Known as the Five Treasures of the Snows because of its five summits, Kangchenjunga is the world's third highest peak (8586m). The trek to base camp is regarded by many as the most beautiful walk in the world. Various options are described by one of the best of current guide book writers. *ISBN 1 85284 280 6 184pp*

LANGTANG, GOSAINKUND & HELAMBU - A Trekker's Guide *Kev Reynolds* Popular area, easily accessible from Kathmandu. *ISBN 1 85284 207 5*

OTHER COUNTRIES

MOUNTAIN WALKING IN AFRICA 1: KENYA *David Else* Detailed route descriptions and practical information. *ISBN 1 85365 205 9 180pp A5 size*

OZ ROCK - A Rock Climber's Guide to Australian Crags *Alastair Lee* An overall view of Oz rock with details of each crag and how to get there. *ISBN 1 85284 237 7 184pp A5 size*

TREKKING IN THE CAUCAUSUS *Yuri Kolomiets & Aleksey Solovyev* The great mountains once hidden behind the Iron Curtain. 62 walks of which half demand basic climbing skills. Included are the walks to the highest tops in Europe, the summits of Mt Elbrus. *ISBN 1 85284 129 X 224pp PVC cover*

ROCK CLIMBING IN HONG KONG *Brian J. Heard* Great climbing for both locals and travellers. *ISBN 1 85284 167 2 136pp A5 size*

TREKKING IN THE CAUCAUSUS *Yuri Kolomiets & Aleksey Solovyev* The great mountains once hidden behind the Iron Curtain. 62 walks of which half demand basic climbing skills. Included are the walks to the highest tops in Europe, the summits of Mt Elbrus. *ISBN 1 85284 129 X 224pp PVC cover*

THE GRAND CANYON and the American South-West *Constance Roos* The long awaited walking and trekking guide to this spectacular region. With clear mapping, superb photographs of the breathtaking scenery and extensive information. *ISBN 1 85284 300 4*

ADVENTURE TREKS WESTERN NORTH AMERICA
Chris Townsend ISBN 1 85223 317 6 160pp large format

CLASSIC TRAMPS IN NEW ZEALAND *Constance Roos* The 14 best long distance walks in both islands. Each "tramp" takes between 2-7 days. ISBN 85284 118 4 208pp PVC cover

NOTES

Get ready for take off

Adventure Travel helps you to go outdoors over there More ideas, information, advice and entertaining features on overseas trekking, walking and backpacking than any other magazine - guaranteed. Available from good newsagents or by subscription - 6 issues £15

Adventure Travel Magazine T:01789-488166

IF YOU LIKE ADVENTUROUS ACTIVITIES ON
MOUNTAINS OR HILLS
YOU WILL ENJOY

Climber

MOUNTAINEERING / HILLWALKING /
TREKKING / ROCK CLIMBING /
SCRAMBLING IN BRITAIN AND ABROAD

*AVAILABLE FROM NEWSAGENTS,
OUTDOOR EQUIPMENT SHOPS,
OR BY SUBSCRIPTION
(6-12 MONTHS) from*

WARNER GROUP PUBLICATIONS PLC
THE MALTINGS, WEST STREET, BOURNE, LINCS PE10 9PH
Tel: 01778 393313 Fax: 01778 394748
ISDN: 01778 423059 email: Sam.a@warners.co.uk

mountain / sports incorporating 'Mountain INFO'

Britain's liveliest and most authorative magazine for mountaineers, climbers and ambitious hillwalkers. Gives news and commentary from the UK and worldwide, backed up by exciting features and superb colour photography.

OFFICIAL MAGAZINE

Have you read it yet?

Available monthly from your newsagent or specialist gear shop.

Call 01533 460722 for details

BRITISH
MOUNTAINEERING
COUNCIL

THE WALKERS' MAGAZINE

THE GREAT OUTDOORS

**COMPULSIVE MONTHLY READING FOR
ANYONE INTERESTED IN WALKING**

*AVAILABLE FROM NEWSAGENTS,
OUTDOOR EQUIPMENT SHOPS, OR BY SUBSCRIPTION
(6-12 MONTHS) from*

**CALEDONIAN MAGAZINES LTD,
6th FLOOR, 195 ALBION STREET, GLASGOW G1 1QQ
Tel: 0141 302 7700 Fax: 0141 302 7799
ISDN No: 0141 302 7792 e-mail: info@calmags.co.uk**

EXPLORE THE WORLD
WITH A CICERONE GUIDE

Cicerone publishes over 280 guides for walking, trekking, climbing and exploring the UK, Europe and worldwide. Cicerone guides are available from outdoor shops, quality book stores and from the publisher.

Cicerone can be contacted on
Tel. 01539 562069
Fax: 01539 563417
www.cicerone.co.uk